T0379588

BECOME TIME RICH

BECOME TIME RICH

HOW TO STOP BEING BUSY AND START GETTING WEALTHY

LLOYD J. ROSS

WILEY

Published by John Wiley & Sons, Inc., Hoboken, New Jersey.
Published simultaneously in Canada.

For general information on our other products and services or for technical support, please contact our Customer Care Department within the United States at (800) 762-2974, outside the United States at (317) 572-3993 or fax (317) 572-4002.

Wiley also publishes its books in a variety of electronic formats. Some content that appears in print may not be available in electronic formats. For more information about Wiley products, visit our web site at www.wiley.com.

Library of Congress Cataloging-in-Publication Data

Names: Ross, Lloyd J. author
Title: Become time rich : how to stop being busy and start getting wealthy / Lloyd J. Ross.
Description: Hoboken, New Jersey : John Wiley & Sons, Inc, [2025] | Includes index.
Identifiers: LCCN 2025003878 (print) | LCCN 2025003879 (ebook) | ISBN 9781394337514 (cloth) | ISBN 9781394337538 (adobe pdf) | ISBN 9781394337521 (epub)
Subjects: LCSH: Time management | Wealth
Classification: LCC BF637.T5 R67 2025 (print) | LCC BF637.T5 (ebook) | DDC 650.1/1—dc23/eng/20250321
LC record available at https://lccn.loc.gov/2025003878
LC ebook record available at https://lccn.loc.gov/2025003879

Cover Design: Wiley
Cover Image: © alexyndr/stock.adobe.com

SKY10101903_040525

This book is dedicated to my mentorship students. Every week, they continue to impress me with their personal growth and achievements. Their inspiration motivates me to pursue ongoing self-improvement, urging me to reach new heights and broaden my own horizons. Like iron sharpening iron, their presence drives our collective progress forward.

Contents

Foreword

The first time I saw Lloyd was at a conference. I walked into a room of over five thousand people where he held the audience captivated. My first impression was "This bloke is a class act." Later that night, I watched on as he was awarded Man of the Year at the same conference.

I knew I had to find out if he was the real deal, so a little later I reached out to Lloyd and suggested we meet up for two reasons. First, to see if he was the real deal, and second, to show him my boxing program. Later that week, we ended up in the boxing ring. At the end of the second round, my first question was answered. He had been tested, and he was definitely the real deal.

He said, "What do you want from me? Do you want me to recommend men to this program?"

I laughed and said, "No, I want you to fight in a men-only fight club in eight weeks in the basement of a nightclub."

Of course, Lloyd said yes, as he does to any worthy challenge, and over the next few months, we endeavored to test his character. At the end of the night, he came out with a win and "Fighter of the Series."

Since that time, we've become best mates. I can honestly say I have witnessed his generosity and willingness to serve others, his incredible integrity, seeing him help other men in our men's group with his natural gift of simplifying what most people find complicated. I have personally tested Lloyd's methods with my own children reading his books and doing his programs. I encourage anybody who wants to achieve more wealth, time freedom, or business growth to follow Lloyd's approach. This book has the ability to change not just your life but the legacy of your family.

—Gavin Lance Topp
Former Australian boxing champion; inductee into the Queensland Boxing Hall of Fame; married, father of seven; creator of Fight Like a Pro and the Man Alive Experience mentorship; author of *A Rite of Passage for the Modern Man* and *Man Alive*

Introduction

As I sat on the edge of my beach chair, sipping my piña colada out of a plastic cup and watching the sun slowly set over the Caribbean Sea, with my wife, Alisha, sitting across from me absorbing the final rays from the Mexican sun, I looked down at my phone and opened my banking app.

Another record month, I thought, mesmerized by the fact that we were making more income in a week than some people make in a year, all while sitting quietly on a beach in Cancun on a three-week jaunt around North America.

In that moment, it was difficult not to feel an overwhelming sense of gratitude and pride for all we'd achieved up to that point and the life we'd built for ourselves over the preceding ten years.

In that time, we'd built, scaled, and were running the following:

- A highly profitable network marketing business (all online) with over 80 consultants globally
- An online education and coaching business that had just been recognized by Clickfunnels.com with a Two Comma Club award

- A successful events business that puts through 400+ students per year across four key events in Australia (so far)
- A company partnership that acquires small, largely automated traditional businesses
- A platform public-speaking business that I run on the side when opportunities emerge throughout the year
- An actively managed, multiple seven-figure equity portfolio that I personally manage
- An award-winning podcast, *Money Grows on Trees*, that's been dropping weekly episodes for three years and counting
- An online social media school

All while traveling to Fiji, Mexico, the United States, Thailand, and Bali.

Not to mention the 35 annual family birthdays (we have a big joint family), business dinners, events to plan, health to look after, a new puppy at home, and the beginnings of starting a family.

How was it possible to manage all of that and still have time to peacefully attack the piece of pineapple living at the bottom of my plastic cocktail cup on a beach in Cancun?

It wasn't magic, nor was it luck. It was the result of a decision made many years earlier to own our time and build a life that would not just grant us a predictable flow of money and financial independence but would also yield a predictable flow of free time to do *whatever* we want, with *whomever* we want, almost *whenever* we want.

It seems ridiculous now to think that you could manage all of the things listed here without having a nervous breakdown, and there was a time in my life when I would have thought it impossible (and certainly unenjoyable) to even consider creating such a plateful.

But there we were, Alisha and I, at peace on the beach, while under the hood of our various enterprises an array of products, people, partnerships, systems, and capital continued working in harmony to produce value for the world in a predictable manner.

As I turned around to look back at the resort, I caught a glimpse of a hammock swaying steadily in the breeze, and I was reminded of the cover of Tim Ferriss's *The Four-Hour Workweek*, a book I'd picked up 12 years prior in a desperate attempt to drastically shift the trajectory of the life I'd found myself in.

But that story takes me back to another exotic location, an island in the Persian Gulf, at a time when my life was *very* different than it is now.

Psychologically Unemployable

As we crossed the bridge onto the island, surrounded by a colossal hotel, theme park, and residential projects under construction, a wave of imposter syndrome washed over me. At the age of 23, fresh out of law school with a few years in real estate sales, I found myself out of my depth, embarking on a job in Abu Dhabi for what was then the sixth-largest development project in the world: Yas Island.

Just a few months earlier, I had been pounding the pavement in Sydney, aspiring to enter the investment banking world. However, the collapse of Bear Stearns and the bankruptcy of Lehman Brothers abruptly halted that pursuit. Amid the global financial crisis, the opportunity to work as an assistant development manager for the world's largest real estate developer in Abu Dhabi felt like a godsend.

Initially, I felt fortunate to contribute to the inaugural F1 Grand Prix circuit and witness a miniature city come to life. However, the aftermath of the Grand Prix brought the financial crisis to the Middle East, and the company I worked for teetered on the brink of bankruptcy. But what truly began to wear me down was the daily three-hour commute to a job that lacked personal growth, career progression, or any real chance for wealth accumulation. In four years, all I encountered were wage cuts, layoffs, and redundancies.

Frustrated by the limitations of a nine-to-five corporate job, I decided to take matters into my own hands. I sought alternative ways to earn money and build wealth, drawing on the knowledge gained from years of reading about money and investing. Despite initial attempts to cut costs and invest in stocks, I soon realized that escaping my job would take a considerable amount of time with this strategy alone. So, I continued my search for a better path.

Listening to audiobooks during my daily commute and reading extensively, I contemplated becoming an entrepreneur.

However, I lacked a clear road map. So instead, I decided to pursue a new career in banking through further studies despite warnings from the financial analysts I worked with.

I committed to the challenging CFA charter program (Chartered Financial Analyst), a self-study program spanning three levels, each with a grueling six-hour, closed-book exam offered only once per year. In 2010, only 90,000 people held this certification worldwide, making it the most prestigious qualification available that would differentiate me in the financial industry. I devoted 20 hours per week and used my annual leave over three years to pass Level I and Level II, and I was on the verge of completing the final level when my career took an unexpected 90-degree turn.

By 2012, the development company had gone through a restructure, and I was moved into a different role, one that required me to do even more wasteful work without increased income or personal growth. At that moment, I came to the realization that I was not cut out for such an existence. I had become "psychologically unemployable."

Getting Out of the Rat Race

About that time, I came across Tim Ferriss's book *The Four-Hour Workweek*, and it resonated deeply with me. It dawned on me that *this* was what I truly yearned for. Not another full-time corporate engagement, not a return to the rat race, the daily grind, or the crucible. What I genuinely craved was control over my own time and agenda. A four-hour workweek. Despite lacking a clear road map, I was certain it must be possible. After all, someone else had achieved it. Why couldn't I?

With that conviction, I sat down at my desk, crafted my resignation letter, and bid farewell to my job in Abu Dhabi. Little did I know that the letter marked the end of receiving a traditional wage. So, with what small amount of money I'd saved, alongside my then girlfriend (now wife), Alisha, I returned to Australia to join my father in a "post-GFC" real estate business, which would quickly become a sink-or-swim ordeal.

What awaited me proved to be one of the most challenging periods of time in my entire career. It seemed like I had a knack for moving to places just as the global financial crisis decimated them. The real estate market was essentially lifeless when I commenced work in March 2012.

Surviving solely on sales commissions, I was grateful for the savings from my previous job, as it took me six months to secure my first deal and make some money. What ensued was a seven-year business baptism by fire. I learned a lot from my dad, and together, we completely reconstructed the property business, discarding unnecessary overhead and debt. We integrated new online systems for greater leverage and repositioned the business away from mortgage reduction into straight property investment planning.

Although I was undeniably earning more than I had in my previous job and I had skilled up tremendously through the many challenges we undertook together, one thing still eluded me. My income, although tied to my performance rather than my time, remained dependent on making sales.

I lacked leverage. What I sought was a four-hour workweek, but what I ended up with was more money and a *six-day* workweek.

Nevertheless, I maintained an open mind, believing that something good would eventually emerge.

It was during this time of rebuilding the property business with my dad that my older sister, Brooke, presented me with an opportunity to create some additional income. This opportunity required minimal time to begin because it would leverage the small social media network I had already built on Facebook, and it was something I could run from my phone in between appointments at work or from home.

At the time, I didn't fully grasp that she was talking about network marketing, but frankly, I didn't care. I wanted time freedom and was willing to do whatever it took to get it. Without any formal training or much knowledge of how to proceed, Alisha and I teamed up with my sister, and we jumped in headfirst. We wholeheartedly embraced the notion of "ignorance on fire."

It's often said that if something looks easy, you just haven't done enough research on it yet. This opportunity was a perfect example of that saying. But I innately knew that hard things were often the most worthwhile.

We started slow, but eventually, we made some sales. I vividly recall the feeling of my first pure product sale. I was sitting at a restaurant with old friends, and I checked my banking app to find a $400 deposit. I held up my phone with a big grin and said, "Check this out!"

They asked, "How did you do that?"

I explained that it was some products I'd been using. Some friends had ordered them, and I got paid by the company.

This marked my first experience earning money online with minimal time or effort—a taste of leveraged income. And I craved more. So, each afternoon, Alisha and I dedicated an hour to our new side business, naming it our "hour of power."

We conducted most of our work from our phones, often in the car. I would pick her up from work and drive home by 6:00 p.m., and we would work on the business together until 7:00, after which we would head inside. Because the company we'd partnered with already had systems in place, we didn't need to undertake the heavy lifting of a traditional business. We leveraged the company's existing infrastructure, products, shipping, and auto payments and focused our time and effort primarily on marketing—a task we could do for free using social media and customer referrals.

It took us about three years of evening work and some weekends, but eventually, we scaled it to about $1,800 per week. Because the income was based on product purchases and reorders rather than us trading hours in an office, it became predictable and recurring each week.

This was the breakthrough I had been waiting for—an opportunity to detach our income from our time and step off the hamster wheel of a traditional workweek to craft a life of our own design.

From that point on, my life began to change profoundly. I made the difficult decision to step away from the real estate business, walk away from the final level of my CFA charter, and pursue the vision I had planted in my mind while sitting at my desk in Abu Dhabi eight years earlier.

Do Not Toil to Acquire Wealth

Success has a funny way of compounding, each achievement leading to another. That's precisely what occurred as we scaled our modest online side hustle into a venture that yielded over $1 million in profits. Invitations to speak or train at company events became commonplace, and during one such event at the Brisbane Convention Centre in Australia, where I was addressing six thousand people after being honored with the Man of the Year award, I caught the attention of a chap sitting in the audience by the name of Gavin Topp.

Unbeknownst to me, Gavin was a former Australian boxing champion and had recently been inducted into the Queensland Boxing Hall of Fame. A random message from him piqued my curiosity, leading to a meeting where he shared his boxing program, *A Rite of Passage for the Modern Man*. This initiative aimed to train ordinary men, over ten weeks, for a boxing match.

Little did I know Gavin wanted to test if I truly embodied the essence of Man of the Year; he challenged me to give it a go. Despite the grueling process, I won the fight and continued training with Gavin. Over time, and after a few more adventurous exploits, we became great friends.

During one of our morning runs along the beach, Gavin suggested that I start another business. I was resistant, not wanting to complicate my life further, so I used the common excuse of "I'm too busy."

His response struck a chord: "When did you decide that having more businesses meant you had to be busier?" He pointed out that Tony Robbins, the world-famous transformation coach, managed 70 businesses and questioned why I couldn't do the same. This challenged my existing paradigm, and I realized that I might be playing too small.

Gavin continued the conversation by referencing Proverbs 23:4, "Do not toil to acquire wealth." This biblical verse left me perplexed, as the old paradigm that associates wealth with tireless toil was deeply ingrained in me.

Gavin continued, "If Tony can do it, why can't you?"

This conversation planted a seed of thought and pushed me to reconsider my self-imposed limitations.

It wasn't until I ventured into our second business, in the education space, that the true meaning of this message became clear. Despite having recurring income from our online network marketing business and steady dividend income from our share portfolio, I had hesitated to take on more to make a greater impact and take our wealth to the next level out of a fear that it would make me "too busy."

As the saying goes . . .

"If the Devil can't make you sin, he'll make you busy."

I certainly wanted to avoid jumping back into the very same rat race I had worked so hard to escape.

I mistakenly believed I had to do everything myself, limiting the potential for further wealth building. Once I realized this and set that old belief aside (as best I could), I carved out some capital to begin a partnership with Gavin's son Jay, and we started and scaled an online education business from scratch, right at the start of the COVID-19.

Scaling this new education business prompted a rapid reevaluation of my time management strategies and my own beliefs about hard work, time, and money. This process led me to identify four underlying laws that, once applied, allowed me to transcend "overwhelm," break free from the shackles of busyness, and embrace true wealth.

But let me be clear. I'm not suggesting that you can do zero work and get rich, and I'm not suggesting it's all smooth sailing. What I can tell you is that if you choose to consistently apply the four laws in this book to your life, I'm confident you won't just become rich; more importantly, you'll become time rich.

Why I Wrote This Book

> *"There comes a point where we need to stop just pulling people out of the river. We need to go upstream and find out why they're falling in."*
>
> —Desmond Tutu

For more than a decade, I have been providing coaching and mentorship to individuals in the realms of finance and business, and over that time I've made an interesting discovery.

Contrary to common belief, most financial challenges people face don't actually stem from a lack of financial intelligence.

Fundamentally, money involves basic arithmetic, perhaps with a sprinkle of primary school math, but it's far from rocket science (fortunately). So what tends to hinder people?

Through numerous discussions and mentoring sessions with my students, a distinct pattern emerged. I uncovered the reasons why, or more precisely *how*, they were falling into the river of financial turmoil. Surprisingly, it wasn't solely due to a deficiency in financial IQ. Rather, I found that the core issue leading to their financial chaos was their inability to effectively manage their time.

I was providing them with straightforward money management systems, educating them on investment principles, and offering practical steps to generate additional income, but these strategies made no impact if they couldn't put them into action due to a lack of motivation, being trapped in procrastination, or experiencing anxiety and overwhelm from taking on too much without the necessary tools or habits to navigate such situations.

However, it wasn't solely the challenge of time management that hindered their capacity to enhance their wealth; it was their mindset and perception of *the relationship between money and time*. Despite recognizing their time as the most valuable commodity on earth, they consistently prioritized money over everything else even at the expense of their happiness.

A significant majority found themselves trading their time in jobs they detested, all in the pursuit of financial gain. The perceived security of a job held such prominence for them that they exchanged their precious time on earth for it. However, when presented with the opportunity or, more accurately, when they granted themselves permission to break free from those jobs, release the burdensome mortgage, and begin investing their time *before* their money, a palpable sense of self-imposed weight lifted from their shoulders.

I had been trying to educate individuals about money and finances while they struggled with time management. It felt akin to applying a Band-Aid to a broken leg. To assist them in expanding their wealth, I realized I had to first aid them in expanding their time—a skill I had taken for granted in my own wealth-building journey.

Reflecting on my own ability to manage time effectively, I recognized that it wasn't merely common sense but a result of crucial mentorship lessons and four distinct laws that I'd adhered to over the years that enabled me to be effective with my time—to achieve more by actually doing less.

These principles, when applied, have enabled me to achieve exceptional financial and lifestyle outcomes that I'm confident you aspire to achieve as well. This book encapsulates those lessons and laws, which I now wish to share with you.

Following them will not only help you scale your time but will subsequently contribute to scaling your wealth. There have certainly been moments in my journey when I've questioned the pursuit of riches, deeming it a costly sacrifice. Nevertheless, as you will come to understand within the pages of this book, I have never swayed from my resolute commitment to become "time rich."

After all, what value does a gold Rolex hold if its only function is to remind you when your lunch break is over?

Wishing you nothing but financial peace,

Lloyd

Chapter 1

The Origins of Busyness

"If the Devil cannot make you sin, he'll make you busy."
—Corrie ten Boom

Growing up in Australia, I often heard the common adage, "If you want a job done well, you have to do it yourself." This principle is deeply rooted in our culture, reflected in the tendency of the typical Australian worker to proudly proclaim, "I'm busy," when asked about their well-being. This inclination to wear the "busy badge" contributes significantly to our sense of self-worth.

The prevailing belief is that idleness leads to laziness, and laziness is associated with a lower social status. The fear of being perceived as idle propels people to embrace busyness because it is equated with success and self-worth. However, this mindset presents a major problem—it's fundamentally incorrect. Contrary to popular belief, wealth does not reside in constant busyness; otherwise, nurses and construction workers would be the wealthiest people in the world.

In fact, wealth and busyness are often at opposite ends of the spectrum. Numerous individuals around the world, despite working tirelessly, struggle financially and find it challenging to carve out a free minute from their busy schedules. This is precisely why John D. Rockefeller, the wealthiest American in modern history, asserted, "He who works all day, has no time to make money."[1] His words highlight the disparity between busyness and true wealth.

Many of us fall into the trap of perpetual busyness because we have linked our self-worth and social status to it. We mistakenly perceive busyness as synonymous with productivity, but the reality is quite different. To attain wealth, one must actually seek ways to become *less* busy—a paradigm shift that is seldom grasped. Treating "busy" as a virtue leading to success is a complete misconception; in reality, it serves as an obstacle to genuine wealth, making busyness a pathway to poverty.

In the past, wealthy individuals avoided excessive work, engaging more in leisure activities like tennis, yacht lounging, and extravagant parties. However, over time, the perception of wealth shifted, especially with the rise of corporate America. The notion of being busy at all times became synonymous with wealth, replacing the traditional image of leisurely affluent individuals.

An article by Drake Baer on Medium talks about this strange cultural shift in our view of busyness over the last couple of centuries. In particular, he mentions a nineteenth-century economist named Thorstein Veblen, who wrote a formative text called *The Theory of the Leisure Class*. Veblen's view on work and wealth, according to Baer, was as follows:[2]

> Not having to work was supposed to be the reward for having made it .... To be at the top was to be a member of the leisure class, for whom abstaining from productive work was part of the deal. Laboring was "a mark of inferiority" for the upper crusters, Veblen writes, and "to be accounted unworthy of man in his best estate."

The same was true, Baer says, in precapitalist societies. Think about medieval Europe, where "the upper class would occupy its time with palace intrigues and courtly hunts, rather than rising and grinding."

So, when did this change? When did we begin to idolize busyness? According to Baer, the shift really began around the 1960s, when the number of dual-income families began to increase.

By the time we get to the 1980s, we have the overworked, constantly busy Wall Street banker as the wealthy ideal—a complete change from the nineteenth-century image of success.

Although the image of the Wall Street banker may have waned since the 1980s, the association between wealth and constant busyness persists today. Many still view wealth through the same lens as evidenced by the emphasis on "hustling" among the younger generation.

Tim Ferriss's book *The Four-Hour Workweek* challenged this mindset, offering a refreshing perspective that you do not have to be endlessly busy to achieve success.

John D. Rockefeller understood this truth during the Gilded Age, but many are only now realizing it. Being busy does not guarantee wealth; in fact, it might hinder it. Famed tech investor and thought leader Naval Ravikant summed it up perfectly on X when he said, "I do not care how rich you are. I do not care if you are a top Wall Street banker. If somebody has to tell you when to be at work, what to wear and how to behave, you are not a free person. You're not really rich."

Perhaps busyness itself is the problem. Too many folks are working hard to make money rather than working hard to scale their time. Are you ready to break this paradigm?

Time Compounds like Money

Over time, I have observed a pattern in the lives of extremely affluent individuals—they operate at a different pace, seemingly unhurried and deliberate in their actions. These individuals, far from being busy for the sake of busyness, are strategic in their endeavors and fiercely protective of their time. Notably, the more wealth they accumulate, the higher they prioritize their time, adhering to the adage "Time is money."

Consider the habits of renowned superwealthy investor Warren Buffett, who places time above money in his hierarchy of priorities. Although Buffett's financial expertise is widely acknowledged, his lifestyle is equally shaped by his unwavering protection of time. Well known for turning down unnecessary commitments and opportunities, Buffett comprehends the true cost of each minute. Did you know having lunch with Warren Buffett could cost about $5 million per hour, a fee some are willing to pay or even surpass? Clearly, time holds immense value for him.

Contrary to a common misconception, Buffett's vigilance over his time is not a consequence of wealth attainment. He did not wake up one day and decide to commit to fewer things because he had finally achieved financial comfort. Instead, this approach was ingrained in his journey from the outset. Rather than becoming rich first and then learning to manage time, he placed a massive value on time early on, shaping the trajectory of his life and success.

Super wealthy individuals like Buffett comprehend a crucial concept: financial independence hinges on efficient time use. They seek avenues where minimal effort yields the highest financial reward. For Buffett, this meant strategically leveraging people and capital to work for him, freeing him from the traditional work grind.

Buffett first grasped this principle as a young boy. He had figured out how to make money by fishing golf balls out of golf course lakes and reselling them to the local clubhouse. However, he quickly learned that the dirty work of fishing them out was overrated, so he began paying a close friend some of his profits to do it for him. Making money with less effort just made sense to him, even at this early age.

He did a similar thing in his late 20s when he established his first managed fund partnership by asking people he knew to provide him with starting capital so he could invest it on their behalf and share in the profits. He ran the famed Buffett Partnership not in the hustle and bustle of Wall Street but instead from a small sunroom in his own home. Although many are still immersed in corporate life at that age, he was already practicing the principles of a four-hour workweek long before the book was written.

Consider all the years of life, freedom, and flexibility he has enjoyed by fiercely guarding his time and letting his money handle the strenuous work. This behavior, which he first learned as a child, led him to become the world's richest person by the time he was 77 years old.

Most individuals attempt to micromanage their lives, cramming as much activity as possible into every hour, believing it will lead to success. However, truly successful people like Buffett focus on time multiplication. They essentially buy back their time, reclaiming hours of work by enabling people, systems, and capital to handle the workload. This is the well-kept secret of the super wealthy, and the good news is you do not have to wait until you are super wealthy to start practicing it. In fact, to become truly wealthy, you must begin practicing it now.

Flip the Hierarchy

Everyone around the globe has the same 24 hours in a day, so what sets Warren Buffett's hourly value at $5 million, and yours might be valued at $10 (or $20 or $100)? The distinction is not about the quantity of hours—Buffett has no more time in a day than you do. The difference lies in how strategically he uses his time compared to most of us.

This challenges the conventional notion that "time is money," as it introduces a more nuanced perspective: time and money do not hold equal value. In reality, time is *more* precious than money. However, the perpetual cycle of financial struggle that many people find themselves in is often a result of doing the opposite—prioritizing money over time.

This inversion of priorities leads individuals into unfulfilling jobs with lengthy and challenging commutes, perpetuating the cycle of busyness that traps billions of people. The key to breaking free from this trap is to reverse the hierarchy—prioritize time over money. Understanding the true value of an hour enables you to reassess your actual hourly worth and safeguard your time vigilantly.

Time theft is not like an unwelcome home robbery; rather, it often occurs when you willingly invite time thieves into your life. Saying yes to every project and task can lead to overcommitment and diminish the value of your time, so recognizing tasks below your hourly rate and delegating them to capable individuals or systems is crucial.

Delegating tasks is often met with resistance due to control issues and a reluctance to impose on others, but avoiding delegation limits not only personal growth but also the potential growth of others. Embracing Warren Buffett's famed philosophy that "hard work will not kill anyone, but why take the risk?" emphasizes the importance of working intelligently rather than avoiding hard work altogether.

By understanding the true value of your own time, eliminating bureaucracy, working with a definite purpose, delegating wisely, and prioritizing what matters most, you will be able to plug the leaks in your time vessel, multiply your time, and achieve greater wealth with less effort.

To make it simpler for you to apply these ideas to everyday life, I've broken them down into a concise set of key principles. Coined the *Four Time-Rich Laws*, these timeless decrees will collectively pave the way for your success.

Chapter 2

First Law

The Law of Definite Purpose

"If you commit to nothing, you'll be distracted by everything."

—James Clear

In 2019, many personal items that had once belonged to world-famous actor and martial artist Bruce Lee were auctioned off for millions of dollars. Among these possessions, one of the most prized items was a handwritten note. Signed by Bruce Lee and dated January 1969, it was titled "My Definite Chief Aim" and read as follows:

SECRET

My Definite Chief Aim

I. Bruce Lee. will be the first
highest paid Oriental super Star
in the United States. In return
I will give the most exciting
performances and render the best
of quality in the capacity of an
actor. Starting 1970 I will achieve
world fame and from then onward
till the end of 1980 I will have
in my possession $10,000,000. I will
live the way I please and achieve
inner harmony and happiness
SECRET
Bruce Lee
Jan. 1969

I, Bruce Lee, will be the first highest paid Oriental super star in the United States. In return, I will give the most

> exciting performances and render the best quality in the capacity of an actor. Starting 1970, I will achieve world fame and from then onward till the end of 1980, I will have in my possession $10,000,000. I will live the way I please and achieve inner harmony and happiness.[1]

In three years' time, he achieved everything in that note. Now, we all know Bruce Lee died young, in an apparent allergic reaction to medication, but nevertheless, think about how much less he would have accomplished in those few short years if he had not had a "definite chief aim" to direct his decision-making.

You never know how much time you get in this life, so you might as well make it count, right? Why waste more months, more years, in an unfulfilling corporate grind when you could be achieving your definite chief aim, living the way you please, and achieving inner harmony and happiness?

Arnold Schwarzenegger had a similar origin story. According to Arnold, one day when he was a young man, he glanced in a store window in Austria and saw the cover of a magazine depicting Hercules from an upcoming movie. The actor playing Hercules was British bodybuilder Reg Park, three-time winner of the Mr. Universe competition.

When Arnold saw the man's physique, he was amazed. It seemed almost superhuman, so he told himself, "I want to have a body just like that man." And, of course, as we all know, he eventually did. Google Reg Park, then Google Arnold Schwarzenegger and compare. The point is, Arnold suddenly had a clear and definite purpose. He knew what he wanted to achieve. He knew exactly what it would look like. And all of the decisions he made and the actions he took from that point on were intended to get him a body like Reg Park.

Bruce Lee and Arnold Schwarzenegger both identified a definite purpose that they could use to weigh every decision they made and every action they took, and it also gave them an easy way to measure success. This enabled both men to cast aside distractions and focus their time, money, and effort on doing only those things that moved them closer to the goal.

In Arnold's case, achieving his definite purpose of becoming just like Reg Park opened up all kinds of doors to even greater success: seven-time Mr. Olympia, Hollywood superstar, and governor of California. Because he was so focused on achieving his definite purpose, he wasn't distracted by anything else. He used his time efficiently by focusing his efforts toward a clearly defined outcome, and when he achieved it and became Mr. Universe, he focused on his next definite purpose: Hollywood superstar.

Rediscovering My Definite Purpose

As for me, when I was working the grind in Abu Dhabi, I mostly just wanted to get on top of my finances and maybe enjoy a little success at work. However, by 2010, my goals and aspirations started to take shape and become a definite purpose. Unlike Bruce and Arnold, I wasn't chasing after Hollywood stardom or the Mr. Universe title. Instead, my focus was twofold.

First, I wanted to accumulate a net worth of $1 million, a goal driven by the allure of living freely off the endless stream of passive income it could provide. Plus, there was something attractive about being able to say, "I have a net worth of a million dollars!" And this aspiration extended beyond mere property holdings. No, I envisioned a *liquid* million, real tangible money that, with the click of a button, was always within my grasp!

Second, I dreamed of being able to craft a life free from the constraints of traditional office life, commuting, and all of the geographical limitations that come with those things.

My vision was clear: I wanted to own my time and somehow gain the ability to work online, unshackled from a fixed location, whether at home or anywhere else in the world, and never again have to ask another human being for permission to go on vacation.

These two objectives formed the core of my definite purpose, a purpose that I committed to paper. Just like Bruce Lee, I wrote a paragraph encapsulating these two goals:

> **What Is Your Why?** My *why* is to ensure that my fiancée no longer has to ask for annual leave and can retire herself from her nine-to-five job where her skills and talents are wasted every day. To ensure that I no longer have to work in my current business every Saturday or write business to create an income each and every month and year. To *help* our friends create financial freedom in their lives. To travel whenever we please. To have a fulfilling mission on this Earth to genuinely help people transform their bodies and their lives through financial freedom.

Ironically, realizing my definite purpose came as a surprise. Years later—in 2018, to be exact—during my transition from the real estate business to full-time online endeavors, I stumbled on an old email containing my definite purpose paragraph while perusing my archives. As I read this beautiful encapsulation of my initial aspirations, I was moved to tears to realize that I had achieved both of my goals: I had a million-dollar net worth and the freedom to work online on my terms. What had seemed like a distant dream when I wrote the paragraph had become my reality within a few short years.

The act of writing down my definite purpose had embedded it into my subconscious, giving me a clarity of purpose that fueled my actions and sustained my motivation. I did not need to depend on "habit stacking" or find some material purchase to motivate me. I was crystal clear about what I wanted: financial success and a free, location-independent lifestyle.

The eight-year journey from that initial inspiration to the tangible realization is a testament to the power of having a definite purpose. I wasn't merely creating distant goals; I was creating a guiding light to steer my actions and maintain my focus. The achievement of my definite purpose marked a profound turning point in my life and, just like Arnold, set the stage for further growth and accomplishment in subsequent years by enabling me to focus my activities and time use toward a specific goal. I wasted far less time on other things, chasing other people's dreams, or trying to figure out what to do next.

Time-Poor Mindset: Living Passively

A business coach once told me that there are two types of people in the world: those who passively receive the world's onslaught and those who confront the world head-on with purposeful intent. That little bit of transformational insight cost me

$20,000, but it was worth the investment because it inspired a personal commitment in me to become someone who seizes control, who shapes and designs life with intention.

I became determined to go *at* the world rather than being at its mercy. That is the essence of a wealth mindset, and it requires you to accept that you have a degree of control over the kind of life you want to lead. Yes, you can consciously design your life by choosing where you live, whom you associate with, and how you spend your time.

This kind of intentional living contrasts sharply with the old "time-poor" mindset of so many people who let external forces dictate their life's course. When you live passively, you become reactive, powerless, and at the mercy of circumstances. Your mindset is mired in impossibility, where decisions are made with a lack of clarity and direction. As a result, a lot of time is wasted because it's not spent with intention. You waste hours, days, or years doing things that do not move you in the right direction toward your dreams.

To escape this old mindset, you must craft a definite purpose that clearly describes what you desire out of life, and then you must accept that you can influence and steer your life toward that desired destination.

People with a time-poor mindset sometimes have big dreams, but they dismiss those dreams as unattainable, convinced that they do not have time to pursue bigger and better things. You have to leave the realm of "impossibility" and move into the realm of "possibility." If someone else can do it, you can do it, too! Accept it, and act accordingly. Make the decision today to pursue *your* dreams, not someone else's.

When I worked that nine-to-five in Abu Dhabi, I was operating within someone else's definite purpose, not my own. The same goes for the real estate business. My work in both of those endeavors was helping someone else achieve their dreams rather than my own. It wasn't until I gained clarity on my own aspirations that I was able to break free from these external influences and pursue my own goals.

To be clear, a definite purpose is not merely a desire for leisure, such as "Someday, I want to be able to sit on the beach all the time." No, it transcends mere relaxation, encompassing how you wish to work, the manner of work you want to do, and the people you want to be surrounded by in your life. It provides a tangible dream that infuses all of your decisions and actions with purpose and eliminates the all-too-common distractions that prey on people who lack a clear direction.

Distractions thrive in the absence of a definite purpose. Easily swayed individuals often find themselves being pulled in multiple directions, saying yes to every invitation, and succumbing to the whims of friends, family, societal expectations, or the demands of daily life. Without a defined path, your daily routine becomes merely a series of reactionary moves, where your dreams get relegated to the background. You are a puppet, and external factors are pulling your strings.

I know this from personal, painful, miserable experience! To break free from this cycle, you must grasp your own strings, pull them with purpose, and navigate life with a vision.

You see, it's not enough to acknowledge the distractions; you also have to create and clarify a definite purpose that will act as a guiding beacon, ensuring that you stay firmly on course.

Time-Rich Mindset: Taking Control

A time-rich mindset approaches life with a sense of control and does not bow to the whims of external forces. People with this mindset take ownership of their destiny, forging a path guided by intentional choices rather than surrendering to the unpredictability of everything around them. Life does not just happen to them; they *make* it happen.

How do they do that? By cultivating a mental map—what we might call a *mind movie*—of their desired life five to ten years in the future. Rather than merely contemplating their aspirations, people with a time-rich mindset have a vivid vision of their desired future, which serves as a source of courage and motivation, propelling them to take uncomfortable yet necessary actions.

The clarity of their mental picture enables them to navigate challenges forcefully, moving toward their goals with determination, and it vastly reduces the amount of time that gets wasted traveling in the wrong direction.

If you do not know where to start in creating your vision of the future, it can be helpful to observe people you admire, just like Arnold Schwarzenegger was inspired by Reg Park. Or, in my case, the way I was inspired by Tim Ferriss and his four-hour workweek.

Look at these inspiring people. Analyze their work, lifestyle, and associations to discover elements or achievements you want to incorporate into your own life. And embrace the notion that if it has been done before, it can be done again.

Once you have clarity about what you hope to achieve, you can begin turning that vision into measurable goals and creating a tangible road map that leads toward your desired future.

Now, having said that, let me be clear: setting and pursuing a definite purpose does not require creating a clear step-by-step plan to get there. Personally, I did not know how I was going to create a net worth of $1 million. I had some basic ideas, but I lacked a concrete plan. Despite this, my mindset was rooted in a certainty that the outcome was possible even if the precise path remained undefined. That's okay. Arnold did not need to know exactly how he was going to develop the muscle-bound physique of Reg Park when he first looked at that magazine cover.

You do not need to possess all the skills, networks, or specific steps from the outset. All you really need is the unwavering belief that your desired destination is attainable. That's all. The objective of your definite purpose is not to meticulously plan every step but to establish and maintain that unwavering motivation and focus on the goal you set.

Why doesn't everyone have a definite purpose? Why do so many people lack a bold vision for what they want to achieve in the future? I think a lot of people have simply never dared to explore their own personal desires. They drift through life on autopilot, conforming to societal expectations and suppressing their own dreams.

A time-rich mindset challenges this passivity. It demands that you declare your aspirations, not merely to survive but to thrive and actively shape the life you desire. Listen to that voice. It is calling you to break free from the shackles of conformity, grant yourself permission to pursue a fulfilling life, and transform the mundane into an extraordinary journey. And by focusing your efforts along that journey, it makes you time rich by guiding your actions on a daily basis.

Cultivating Your Definite Purpose

"That all sounds fabulous, Lloyd, but how exactly can I pinpoint my definite purpose?" It's a question many of us grapple with. Like most people, I spent years unsure of my path, shifting between careers without a clear sense of direction or passion. I possessed various skills but lacked that unmistakable "calling." So I followed Gary Vaynerchuk (famous serial entrepreneur and motivational speaker) and his wisdom of being "80 percent happy" until I realized there was a unique mission awaiting me.

I could not stumble on it; instead, I cultivated it. Setting a concrete goal of attaining financial independence acted as my guiding light, propelling me to expand my horizons. Realizing that the traditional nine-to-five route would not lead me there, I discarded that notion. Instead, I embraced the idea of becoming an investor, recognizing it as a path toward my goal.

I understood that increasing my income necessitated acquiring profitable skills, like sales, marketing, and public speaking. So, I immersed myself in mastering these areas. Moreover, I acknowledged that to achieve financial independence sooner, I needed to establish a scalable business. Thus, I focused my efforts on building such a venture.

Throughout this journey, I gradually unearthed my strengths, tapped into my spiritual gifts, and discovered work that not only resonated with me but also brought immense joy.

I discovered that by expanding my expertise and capabilities, I'd widened the path to finding fulfilling work and making it profitable. Setting a clear mission propelled me toward discovering what I truly loved, which in turn fueled my productivity and satisfaction. When you are engaged in work you love, it does not feel like work at all; you lose track of time, and weekends become irrelevant.

The beauty of having a definite purpose is that it eliminates struggles with focus and motivation. Unlike habits that fluctuate, a definite purpose is unwavering. So, how can you uncover yours? Here are some steps to guide you.

Listen to the Whisper

A critical step to discovering your definite purpose is to listen to the subtle voice of your heart rather than the rational thought in your head. It'll not be a loud calling, but more of a whisper. Whether as a fleeting thought or a soft murmur, the crucial thing is not to dismiss it. Often, this whisper signifies a call to explore a new path. As Robert Greene explains in his book, *Mastery,*[2]

> The first step then is always inward. You search the past for signs of that inner voice or force. You clear away the other voices that might confuse you—parents and peers. You look for an underlying pattern, a core to your character that you must understand as deeply as possible.

Once you hear it, pause and ask yourself, *If I were to pursue this path, what would be my very next move?* This simple question serves as a catalyst for transforming the seemingly impossible into the achievable. Take one step forward, then another, and gradually you'll navigate from the impossible to the possible.

Have Some Fun (Experiment!)

Developing a definite purpose, or what Greene calls "your life's task," can be akin to finding a life partner. You do not just marry the first person you bump into, right? You flirt a bit first to see if you like the person, then you go on a few dates to get to know them more, then after some time you might become engaged, and then you marry them. When carving out your definite purpose, it's wise to flirt with possibilities, date the most promising ones, and ultimately marry the one that resonates deeply. Do not settle until you have found the perfect match.

Choose a Role Model

One pivotal question that guided me in defining my definite purpose was "Whose traits do I wish to embody?" By identifying individuals whose character traits I admired, I gravitated toward mentors whose values, attitudes, and professional pursuits resonated with me the most. Inspired by my father's ambition, skills, and zest for life, I chose to emulate him in mastering sales, entrepreneurship, and cultivating a winning mindset. I've endeavored to embrace my mum's thrift, integrity, and down-to-earth nature to the best of my ability. Similarly, I've drawn inspiration from friends like Gavin Topp, who exemplifies bold living and a commitment to family and adventure. Moreover, figures like Warren Buffett and Charlie Munger influenced my career trajectory and money mindset.

If you are stuck with whom to model in your own circle, then reading books is an exceptional way to find the types of characters you wish to emulate in various ways.

Complete a DISC Profile

I hope you aspire to achieve financial independence as a vital component of your definite purpose. However, it's essential to recognize that our chosen path toward this shared goal may vary due to our specific personality traits.

A DISC profile assessment can illuminate whether you lean toward dominant (D), influential (I), steady (S), or compliant (C) traits. You can easily access a free test online (simply Google "free DISC profile test") to pinpoint your innate strengths. By understanding these natural tendencies, you can tailor your definite purpose to capitalize on your strengths and advantages.

For instance, individuals with high compliance and low dominance and influence may find event management unappealing but excel in building an accounting practice as a business.

Completing this test accelerates the discovery of your inherent talents, guiding you toward work that not only aligns with your mission but also brings you greater fulfillment.

Take a "Spiritual Gifts" Test

Alisha and I recently took a spiritual gifts test through our church. It involved answering a series of questions designed to reveal our natural talents in different areas. Interestingly, I scored low in craftsmanship, which is not surprising, considering I'm not particularly handy. Similarly, both Alisha and I scored low in hospitality, reflecting our infrequent hosting of guests at our home! These results shed light on why I struggled in my previous job in real estate development (construction) and why we rarely organize events ourselves.

However, I scored high in teaching and exhortation (influencing others to take action), which explains my success in running multiple businesses across various industries.

Meanwhile, Alisha excelled in administration and discernment (the ability to judge well), making her invaluable for detail-oriented tasks and providing intuitive insights for major decisions.

Even if you are not particularly spiritual, I highly recommend taking a spiritual gifts test online (just Google "free spiritual gifts test"). Understanding your innate gifts can be a valuable tool in defining your clear, definite purpose and exploiting your unfair advantages.

Have the Uncomfortable Conversation (Take Bold Action)

Ultimately, if you have a definite goal or purpose you are determined to achieve, mere intention will not work unless you are willing to engage in that uncomfortable conversation.

However, from my own experience, the scenarios we concoct in our minds about how these tough discussions will unfold rarely come to pass. More often than not, you'll realize that all of your worries were unfounded and wonder why you hesitated for so long.

One helpful mental exercise for navigating difficult decisions is what I call the *Deathbed Test*. Many individuals have a crystal-clear purpose but hesitate to act on it, fearing it might upset someone or not yield the desired outcome. In such moments, imagine yourself at age 90, lying in a hospital bed, nearing your last breath. When you look back at the decision you are facing now, would your future self make the same choice? Would they take the leap?

This mental exercise has personally guided me through many challenging conversations. Why? Because the pain of regret, imagining myself in that hospital bed, far outweighs the discomfort of having an awkward discussion. Imagine if Bruce Lee wrote down his definite purpose and then did nothing about it.

Law of Definite Purpose Tactics

First tactic: Cultivate a mental map of your desired life five to 10 years in the future. To create this image, dare to listen to the subtle voice in your heart. Maybe flirt with a few possibilities before you settle on one specific vision. When you finally have clarity about your desired future life, this becomes your definite purpose.

Second tactic: Analyze the work, lifestyle, and associations of someone you admire, someone who has achieved a lifestyle similar to the one you have envisioned for yourself. Discover elements of their success or achievements that you want to incorporate into your own life.

Third tactic: Begin creating measurable goals and a tangible road map to get to your desired future. You may also complete a DISC profile assessment or a "spiritual gifts" test to help determine the road ahead. Be willing to have difficult conversations and take bold action to start moving in the right direction.

Getting Out of Perth

Daniel, one of my mentorship students, began his journey in the distant city of Perth, which is nestled on the western coast of Australia, a vibrant but remote location. When I first began to chat with Daniel on Instagram, he was on the verge of becoming a father, but he felt stuck in a construction job in an industry he despised.

His dream was simple yet profound: he had a fierce desire to escape the closed-mindedness and toxicity of the construction industry and find a more thrilling and lucrative path, possibly in sales. However, he did not have a lot of opportunity to build a new life because he resided on the far side of the country, possessed limited skills, and was about to welcome his first child.

Daniel had plenty of excuses to avoid crafting a definite purpose for a very different life, but despite the excuses, he defied the odds. After our conversation, Daniel took the first step toward transforming his mindset by crafting a clear and definite purpose. He wrote, "I will move to the other side of the country, where opportunities await, and I will transition into sales."

And then he began taking actionable steps to make it happen. He started scouring opportunities in sales outside of the geographical limitations of Perth. When he learned that I live on the Gold Coast, he expressed a desire to relocate there as well. I advised caution, suggesting that he first secure a job and then embark on the move. But Daniel was unfazed. He began searching for both a sales role *and* a place to live at the same time.

Soon, with his wife and newborn child, he made the bold decision to uproot their lives and make the move. Today, Daniel thrives in a sales role and is enjoying an amazing life on the Gold Coast. He is also building an investment portfolio. When I talk to him now, he radiates happiness, and his family is thriving.

This is an example of the transformative power of clarifying your definite purpose. What set Daniel apart was not just his desire to relocate all the way across the continent, nor his intention to change careers, but his courage to take action. He took fearful action, made difficult decisions, and translated his vision into reality. Because he had a definite purpose, he also had unwavering determination to keep moving forward toward the life he truly desired. To that end, he recently joined our crew team for an event we hosted in Sydney with Tai Lopez. That's a long way from the construction industry in just twelve months, wouldn't you say?

Exercise: Creating Your Definite Purpose

Here's how it works:

To become time rich, you have to minimize the distractions that permeate your daily life. The best way to do this is to gain a high degree of clarity about your aspirations by crafting a vision that will act as a shield against the constant onslaught of distractions.

I recommend crafting a one-paragraph essay that describes your desired life five to 10 years from now. This is the definite purpose you are going to work toward. If you do not know where to start, consider the lifestyle and accomplishments of people you admire. Remember, your definite purpose needs to be achievable, but it should also be rather bold. If other people have gone before you and achieved your dream, then you know for sure it's possible even if you do not yet know how to get there.

Your definite purpose will naturally pave the way for the necessary steps to unfold organically, so this is where you need to start. From a definite purpose, you can begin creating clear goals and milestones that will inform your decisions, but it's the purpose that will serve as your motivation to continue taking the right actions.

Look, I know from personal experience how easy it is to get entangled in a web of daily distractions, struggle with motivation, or feel like you just do not have enough time left to improve your life. However, if you have a definite purpose, you can focus on the right things, cast aside the distractions, and redirect all of your energy exclusively toward the things that move you in your desired direction. This is how you begin to liberate yourself from the time constraints that keep you from achieving your time-rich life.

Once you have finished, the next crucial step is to ruthlessly eliminate as many distractions as possible so as not to hinder progress toward your definite purpose.

> If you would like some help implementing the Law of Definite Purpose, head to the back of the book and click the link or scan the QR code to book a free Time Rich coaching session with our team.

Chapter 3

Second Law

The Law of Elimination

"Never organize what you can discard."

—Joshua Becker

The journey to success is usually seen as a process of accumulating all of the right elements in your life although I think a more apt analogy would be comparing it to sculpting a masterpiece. In other words, it's a process of chiseling away everything that is extraneous, not piling on more and more material. It's a principle of subtraction over addition, removing the nonessential components from your life, not adding more stuff.

There's an old legend told about the Renaissance artist Michelangelo and his famous marble sculpture of David. On viewing the masterpiece, an admirer approached the artist and asked him, "How did you create this incredible work of art?"

And Michelangelo replied, "I simply removed the parts that weren't David."

The story is almost certainly apocryphal, but it makes an important point. Creating time for yourself almost always involves the meticulous elimination of elements that don't align with your definite purpose.

I call this principle the *Law of Elimination*, and it is absolutely crucial to cultivating a time-rich life.

There's a great example of this in a story told about Warren Buffett and his private pilot, Mike Flint. Flint was seeking some insight into Buffett's success, so Buffett tasked him with creating a list of the top 25 goals he wanted to accomplish in his life. Mike went to work creating his list, considering it carefully, and he finally brought back the list and showed it to his boss.

Now Buffett said, "Okay, review your list and circle the top five most important priorities."

Mike considered his 25 goals and picked out the five that were most important to him. He circled them in red and showed the list to his boss again.

"Okay, those five things are now your goals," Buffett said.

"What about the ones I didn't circle?" Mike asked. "I should still focus on them intermittently, right?"

"No," Buffett replied. "The 20 goals you didn't circle are to be avoided at all costs. Give them no attention whatsoever. Focus all of your effort exclusively on the ones you circled."

Buffett's own life is a testament to the effectiveness of this approach. Despite his wealth, he hasn't accumulated multiple houses but resides in the same home in Omaha, Nebraska. Why? Because owning a bunch of homes is not one of his primary goals in life, does not add to his happiness, and only creates more obligations. He also says no to all nonessential commitments, guarding his schedule ruthlessly by keeping an organized diary and using a gatekeeper (his assistant, who filters all his inbound calls and messages).

He deliberately eliminates all nonessentials from his life, whether material possessions or commitments. This is the essence of the Law of Elimination, and it's one of the primary reasons why he has enjoyed enduring success.

Like Buffett, you have to discern which life events, goals, and experiences contribute to your definite purpose and which do not. Chip away at the ones that don't and get rid of them. Yes, I know this runs counter to the thinking of most people, who are convinced that a fulfilling life is the result of saying yes to everything.

In the beginning of your journey, it's important to embrace a lot of opportunities so you can determine what your purpose is, but once your purpose is defined, the key is to say no to every opportunity that doesn't contribute to it.

Saying yes to everything does not lead to a fulfilling life—not for anyone. In the end, you just feel inundated and strung out. Fulfillment comes from the transformative power of eliminating the unnecessary and focusing only on the essential. Every time you say yes to something, you say no to everything else. If you want to live a truly successful and purposeful life, you have to start getting rid of all the little bits and pieces that don't contribute to the masterpiece.

Chipping Away at My Life

I discovered the Law of Elimination firsthand when I found myself working six days a week in our property business and using time between clients (and most evenings) to build our network marketing business, while at the same time studying 20 hours a week for my Level III CFA charter exam *and* prepping for my first ever natural bodybuilding competition. To say I was "busy" would have been a true understatement.

Clearly, I had overcommitted myself. But due to my desire for significance and self-worth, I found it extremely difficult to "quit" things. After all, my identity was that of someone who never walked away from a challenge because "successful people don't quit things." This deeply ingrained identity made it increasingly difficult to drop even one of the several large plates I was spinning. I tried as best I could to ignore the inner voice that was desperately telling me to let go, but eventually, it all caught up with me.

One afternoon, on the weekend, I sat down and flipped open my CFA textbook, titled *Options Derivatives*. Exhausted from the week that had just passed, I finally said to myself, *Enough! Something has got to give here, Lloyd. You can't go on like this.*

It was a war inside my head ...

You can't quit now; you've come so far.

You'll regret it. You've never walked away from anything you started.

What will people think of you if you quit at the final turn?

These voices were the loudest, but beneath all of them, I heard a different voice, little more than a whisper, saying, "You can't do it all, not if you expect to do anything well. Follow your heart, Lloyd. Go after your definite purpose. This no longer fits into the game plan."

It was true. I simply could not afford to spend 20 hours a week pursuing something that didn't move me toward my goals, but it was hard to let go. I was five years into the CFA program, and I'd already used up my annual leave, a vast amount of financial resources, and a ton of time. I stood on the precipice of completion with only one exam remaining in the CFA program.

It didn't matter. I knew I couldn't logically sustain the exhausting schedule. I spent about six months weighing the decision until a serendipitous encounter changed my perspective. A woman named Peta Kelly shared her story on stage at a marketing event, recounting her difficult decision to abandon her pursuit of a PhD just before completion. Her rationale mirrored my own internal struggle. She realized it no longer aligned with her definite purpose.

It's really hard to get rid of something you've invested so much into, even more so when it has held so much personal significance for you. Peta Kelly was on the verge of being able to call herself a doctor. What an honor! I was on the verge of being able to call myself a Chartered Financial Analyst. However, true liberation comes when you free yourself from constraints that impede your progress no matter how much investment, honor, or glory might come along with them.

So, after what seemed like a six-month war in my head over which avenue to take, which "project" to eliminate, I set my heart on letting go of my CFA charter designation. After studying for five long years, using evenings, weekends, and annual leave to study for over a 2,000 hours, I made the very tough decision to walk away from one of the most coveted financial qualifications in the world—one exam shy of completion—to ultimately save my sanity and win back my time.

As my mind made the final decision, I could feel the heavy burden of this commitment that I'd carried for so long lift off my shoulders. A sense of freedom washed over me. I had made my first substantial decision to eliminate something that did not fully support my definite purpose, and it felt great.

How did I finally make that final decision?

In hindsight, it made logical sense. After all, I was a small business owner who had dreams of scaling an online business to create recurring income and buy assets that would secure my financial independence (to do what I wanted, when I wanted).

Essentially, my definite purpose was leading me in a very different direction, a direction that made a CFA charter largely irrelevant, so I figured my time was better spent developing the business vehicle that was sure to get me to where I wanted to go rather than securing yet another academic qualification.

What happened as a result of making this difficult decision to eliminate something with such high perceived importance?

It gave me more time to actually build my online business, which, as a result, flourished.

Within two years of that fateful decision, I won my first natural bodybuilding competition, and Alisha and I catapulted our online health business to a multiple six-figure recurring annual profit. It turned out that my heart, my gut, and eventually my brain had been correct in applying the Law of Elimination.

When I say "eliminate everything," I'm not saying you should get rid of your family or abandon your parental responsibilities—not at all. You still have moral obligations that you need to keep, like being a good parent or a faithful spouse. Rather, I'm suggesting you cast aside all projects that impede your purpose, even the things that hold immense personal significance or investments of time, effort, and sentiment.

Yes, it's daunting, and that's why many individuals don't do it. They hold on to time sinks that keep them from unlocking additional time and reaching their goals because they've attached an unnecessary amount of emotion or identity to those things.

So, maybe it's time to have a brutally honest conversation with yourself. Maybe it's time to admit that there are some things you've poured a lot of time, effort, and emotion into that just need to be set aside. My CFA charter wasn't the only thing I had to eliminate from my life. As my online business flourished and my investment portfolio grew—both contributing to my million-dollar definite purpose—I realized I also had to get out of the property business.

I first got involved in real estate with my dad because we were trying to resurrect a family business that had been hit hard by the global financial crisis. So, there was a lot of emotion and family history tied to the business. It wasn't just about the money. For seven years, Dad and I toiled side by side, bringing the family business back to life like a phoenix rising from the ashes. Yet, in my heart, I knew my path lay elsewhere.

As our online health business flourished, I was once again faced with another difficult decision: to stay in our property business and attempt to grow two businesses at once or to let one go and focus solely on the business that best supported my definite purpose.

Elimination is not easy when you have to disappoint someone in the process. When I faced the decision to walk away from my CFA charter, the only person I had to let down was me, but when faced with the prospect of leaving our family property business, it was a far more heart-wrenching decision.

I've often said success is largely achieved by having one uncomfortable conversation after another: a tough sales conversation, an emotional conversation to break up with a partner in a bad relationship, or a difficult conversation to apologize and mend a bridge. These types of conversations require the most courage because there is often so much at stake. Nobody wants to be disliked, unloved, or disrespected—quite the opposite. And that's why we try so fervently to avoid such confrontational conversations.

But this is also why avoiding them often leads to less success, less wealth, and in many cases, much less time. The conversation I knew I had to have with my dad was no different. What was he going to say? How was he going to feel? Would the family business be okay without me? What if he talked me into staying?

I knew it was going to be hard, but I also knew that it wouldn't be as hard as living with the regret that I'd followed someone else's dream instead of my own. It takes courage to sing the song in your heart. As Fumitake Koga says in his bestselling book, "It takes courage to be disliked."[1] So with that in mind, I asked my dad if I could have a chat with him downstairs, outside the office.

As I stood against the concrete balustrade, I summoned up three seconds of courage and just went for it, blurting out "I think I'm going to go full-time into our online business, Dad. I don't feel I have the time to succeed with it if I stay in the property business, too."

And you know how he responded?

"I know, mate. You have to do what you want to do. I would be more disappointed if you felt this way and didn't follow your heart."

And just like that, all the horror stories I'd conjured up in my head didn't happen. I mean, I know my dad well and we are very close, so I knew he wasn't going to blow his top, but still, I was surprised at how well he took it. Looking back at that conversation, I have no doubt it must have been crappy news to receive. His own son was basically bailing on him, but he knew I would not have made that decision lightly.

Ironically, the most interesting thing happened after I left the property business. Not only did our online business and wealth creation boom (due to the extra time and freedom to focus on it) but so did my dad's property business! In fact, after I left, he made a critical pivot and subsequently experienced some of his most profitable years.

It just goes to show you that when you have the courage to follow your own definite purpose and shine your own light, it gives others the chance to do the same.

With these two monumental decisions now behind me, I was becoming accustomed to having hard conversations to free up my time, deeply embedding the power and significance that comes from applying the Law of Elimination.

Time-Poor Mindset: Seizing Every Opportunity

According to science, the human brain makes about 35,000 conscious decisions a day.[2] That's a lot, but it's still finite. And time-poor people squander those finite decisions on things that don't propel them toward their definite purpose. Why do we do this?

There are three core drivers of human behavior, three innate "needs" that make us do what we do. The first is a need to increase our sense of self-worth. The second is a need to increase our sense of significance in the world. And the third is a need to increase our feeling of security and safety.

We try to seize every opportunity that comes our way in an attempt to satisfy one or more of these core human needs. As a result, we want to do everything and experience everything, take on every project that crosses our path so we don't miss out. It sounds like a grand plan in theory, but consider the harsh reality. More often than not, we find ourselves making a lot of unfulfilled promises to other people. The list of things we never get around to is as vast as the ocean.

Our lives can become a battlefield of missed project deadlines, checklists full of exotic destinations we hope to visit someday (but probably never will), and accomplishments never fully realized because there's never enough time. At a deeper level, we are afraid to say no because we're scared to let people down, and we lack the courage to be disliked. So we play the rescuer, tirelessly putting everyone else's oxygen mask on while neglecting our own needs, only to bemoan the lack of time afterward.

In self-imposed chaos, the poor soul suffers from decision fatigue due to a constant barrage of choices. And what do we wind up with after all of that struggle? Too many jobs; too many side hustles; too many investments of shares, property, gold, foreign exchange, and Bitcoin; and an exhausting array of unrealized aspirations. Essentially, we let small opportunities cheat us out of big possibilities.

Time-Rich Mindset: Less Is More

What's the antidote to this chaos? The minimalist architect Ludwig Mies van der Rohe figured it out in the nineteenth century when he popularized the phrase "Less is more." That's the antidote right there. It reminds me of a line a friend of mine once told me, "Lloyd, you can't dance at every wedding."

Think of all of the decisions you make in a day as fuel in a "decision tank." Part of becoming time rich is being cautious not to drain the tank recklessly on tasks that don't align with your definite purpose. Otherwise, you'll run out of fuel before you get where you truly want to go.

The "less is more" mentality stands in stark contrast to the chaotic thinking of our time, but it is the way forward. The minimalists had another helpful saying: "No is a complete sentence." That is a time-rich mindset.

I know it's challenging, but you must summon the courage to disappoint others, especially when every fiber in you and everything you've ever known screams at you, "Don't!" When you feel this way, you must somehow find the courage to shift just a little, just once—that's all it takes—and then you'll feel something wonderful that you can't unfeel: liberation.

Recognize that success often requires a series of uncomfortable conversations, just like the one I had with my dad. I really didn't want to let him down, but doing so was a pivotal moment in my journey. You might have to disappoint yourself as well. That's what

I did when I abandoned the CFA charter, but in doing so, I shed the weight of a legacy that no longer aligned with my purpose.

When it comes to commitments, Alisha and I play this little game we call "Hell Yes or No." Every potential distraction, task, or event invitation we receive that does not elicit a resounding "Hell yes!" from us is automatically a firm no. This ensures that our commitments always align with our passions.

A mentor of mine used to guard his time ruthlessly by inserting the word *something* in his electronic calendar. That way, whenever he was faced with an invitation or request that he didn't particularly wish to fulfill, he could honestly say, "I already have *something* in my diary." It was a subtle yet effective way to manage commitments and protect his precious time.

The time-rich mindset champions the elegance of *less* over the chaos of *more*, embracing the power of a well-placed no and a strategic yes. The Law of Elimination becomes a deliberate choice to curate a life that resonates with purpose, not busyness.

Law of Elimination Tactics

First tactic: Muster the courage to "disappoint" someone. Have that difficult conversation you've been avoiding. Send that text. Make that call. Or arrange that meeting you know you have to have.

Second tactic: Apply the "Hell Yes or No" game to an activity or invitation you're contemplating this month. See how it feels.

Third tactic: Put the word *something* in your digital calendar and use it when asked by someone to do something you truly do not wish to do.

Pamela's Resignation

When I first started mentoring Pam, she had found herself immersed in a sea of responsibilities. I could tell she was struggling, so I recommended that she try a version of Warren Buffett's "Five out of Twenty-Five" exercise. In the span of 30 seconds, I had her jot down the top 10 tasks that were currently demanding her time and attention. She quickly listed them all.

Then, after a 10-second pause, I told her to mercilessly strike out all but three items on the list. The objective was clear: to distill her focus to a manageable trio. In my experience, the human mind can only really grapple with three priorities at a time. Warren Buffett prefers five, but I think when we move beyond three, our thoughts tend to start spiraling out of control.

As Pam feverishly crossed out seven tasks, she did something rather remarkable. She scratched out her job! This led to a deeper conversation afterward where she realized that her job was a distraction from her real desire. She wanted to build her own business—that was her dream—but she was hindered from doing so by the comforting constancy of her regular full-time career.

"Maybe I should find a way to quit my job in six months," she said.

I made a bolder proposition. "Why don't you do it tomorrow?"

The suggestion caught her off guard. The job was a kind of security blanket in her life, but it was keeping her from moving toward her real purpose. It had to go!

"Write your resignation letter today," I said.

To my surprise, she embraced the idea and promptly drafted the letter. Within a few weeks, she was out of that job and transitioning into a full-time commitment to her business, where she now confidently owns her time, paycheck, and workload.

You see, it's not just stress and obligations that hold us back. Sometimes, it's the allure of a secure paycheck, the fear of disappointing your boss, the desire to accumulate tasks, or the comfort of being busy that keeps us from moving in the right direction. These time-poor behaviors, emotions, and unimportant tasks cling to us like chunks of marble covering Michelangelo's statue of David, and they need to be chipped away, no matter how comforting they may be.

Chipping away the unnecessary must become a continual practice because it's the only way to distill our focus, refine our purpose, and win back our time.

As Naval Ravikant famously admitted on X, "Time is the ultimate currency and I should have been more tight-fisted with it."

Exercise: Refine Your Focus

Here's how it works:

- Write a list of the top 10 things you are currently working on—that means the top 10 projects and tasks that demand your direct time and attention. Do it quickly, within 30 seconds. Don't overthink it.

- Once you're done, pause for 10 seconds (no longer than ten). Then cross out seven things on the list, leaving only the three most important things.
- The seven things you crossed out are tasks and obligations that need to be chipped away from your life. Focus on the three!

This is a good way to begin practicing the Law of Elimination. Obviously, it may be hard to get rid of some of these things, but I promise it will set you free. In fact, there's a lot more we can say about eliminating "stuff" from your life, so let's spend a little more time exploring it in the next chapter.

Chapter 4

The Elimination of Stuff

"It feels better to do stuff than to have stuff."

—Joshua Becker

As we've already discussed, the Law of Elimination is about getting rid of nonessential tasks, commitments, meetings, and events in order to free up your time to focus on higher-value things. But here's the thing: if you want to experience true freedom, you also need to get rid of a lot of the material "stuff" that clutters up your life.

Yes, I know this recommendation runs contrary to the general view of affluence. Most people think being wealthy means owning a lot of stuff—vehicles, vacation homes, yachts, cars, jewelry, and so on. What do you do when you make a lot of money? You buy a lot of nice, expensive stuff. That's the whole point of being rich, isn't it? As the old saying goes, "He who dies with the most toys wins."

Actually, no, that's a time-poor mindset, especially in the modern age. Look, in the long-ago past, people who owned the most stuff had the most resources, and that made them both wealthy and influential. They could barter those resources with other people, which gave them incredible power and position in society. But in our world of abundance today, more people have access to basic resources than ever before.

Ordinary people don't need to barter with the lord of the manor to get the resources they need to survive a tough winter. Consequently, most of the kinds of things that rich people buy today aren't necessary. They are indulgences driven by faulty thinking because we've gotten ownership mixed up with abundance.

But as Morgan Housel, author of the book *The Psychology of Money: Timeless Lessons on Wealth, Greed, and Happiness*, puts it, "Money's greatest intrinsic value—and this can't be overstated—is its ability to give you control over your time."[1] Whom you spend time with and what you spend your time doing are far more important than accumulating a bunch of expensive stuff that's going to demand your constant attention.

Time-Poor Mindset: Wealthy People Own Stuff

The time-poor mindset says, "I must own a lot of stuff because wealthy people own a lot of stuff." The problem is, when you own something, whether it's a vehicle, a vacation home, a boat, or something else, you have to maintain it. You have to pay for its upkeep and storage, for maintenance and repairs, or whatever else. Additionally, you feel guilty if you don't use it. I can't tell you how many people I've known who bought vacation homes and then felt bad that they were too busy to use them. Or they bought a second, third, or fourth car and then felt guilty that they rarely drove it.

If you feel obligated to use something just because it's costing you money, then that thing owns you as much as you own it. As Winston Churchill said, "We shape our buildings; thereafter they shape us."[2] The same could be said of our material possessions. People's lives end up being constrained and limited by all the possessions they've accumulated. They don't just fill up their garage, storage shed, and closets, they fill up their week with noncritical administrative tasks and their head with the feeling of guilt from not using them. That's not freedom.

Personally, one of the only things I want to own is cash flow. Everything else becomes restricting.

I recall sitting on a yacht off the coast of Thailand with Alisha, my dad, and his partner. We sipped drinks, sat in lounge chairs, and watched the sun set. It was an amazing experience, part of an epic around-the-world adventure that took us to Bali, Cancun, Miami, Orlando, Fiji, and many other places. But here's the thing: I didn't own the yacht. I rented it. If I owned it, I'd have to take care of it and pay for upkeep, repairs, fuel, storage, and more. I'd feel guilty if I didn't use it enough because I'd sunk so much money into it.

By renting it, I got all the benefits with none of the guilt or obligation. Why do I need to own it anyway? Because rich people are supposed to own yachts? That's not a good enough reason for me, not when it could limit my freedom and flexibility.

Warren Buffett has lived in the same home for 70 years. He doesn't own multiple houses all over the world even though common wisdom says that's what super wealthy people are supposed to do. His business partner, Charlie Munger, was the same way. He lived in the same house for decades.

According to Buffett, they noticed early on that all of their friends who got wealthy started buying multiple nice homes, but as their homes became more expensive and more numerous, their happiness didn't seem to increase. This has been my experience as well. Buying more (and more expensive) stuff doesn't seem to make people happier. It just gives them more to worry about.

Even Elon Musk, the wealthiest man in the world, wound up selling all of his homes and assets and is living on-site at SpaceX in a small, simple building. Less clutter in his life means a less cluttered mind, and after all, his ideas are more valuable to him and to the world than owning a few homes.

Even beyond the financial cost of upkeep and storage, there's the mental cost of owning more stuff. Remember, the human brain can only make a finite number of decisions in a day. Anytime you buy something, you are also buying a series of future decisions you will have to make about it, which takes you one step closer to decision fatigue. Conversely, every time you get rid of something, you're also eliminating a certain number of future decisions you would have to make.

In fact, that's a good way to look at it. You're not just eliminating stuff; you're eliminating future decisions. The fewer decisions you have to make, the more time you free up for yourself.

It's been rumored that Mark Zuckerberg wears the same-colored shirt every day. Why? So he doesn't have to decide what to wear when he gets up in the morning. That's one less decision to worry about. Because he's not into fashion, selecting clothes is not an important decision for him, so he has eliminated it from his daily routine. Save your time and energy for the most important decisions.

Burdened with Nice Stuff

Long before I started in business with my dad, I would often visit his office during school holidays. On one occasion, as I sat in one of the Chesterfield chairs across from his sprawling mahogany desk, I watched as he opened a plethora of envelopes addressed from the Department of Transport.

- "Registration due for the Porsche 911."
- "Registration due for the Austin-Healey."
- "Registration due for the Jet Ski."

- "Registration due for the Jet Ski trailer."
- "Registration due for the Range Rover."
- "Registration due for the boat."
- "Registration due for the boat trailer."
- "Registration due for the hot rod."
- "Registration due for the Harley-Davidson."
- "Insurance due for the Porsche 911."
- "Insurance due for the Austin-Healey."
- "Insurance due . . ."
- "Maintenance due . . ."
- "Flat battery . . ."
- Etc. etc. etc.

At one point, he owned eight properties, four classic cars, two prestige cars, three motorcycles, one hot rod, three Jet Skis, a boat, and a 280-acre farm. This had created a mountain of paperwork that he had to wade through, and I could tell it was becoming quite a burden. Not only did he have to spend an inordinate amount of time trying to administer and maintain them all, but he had to constantly try to figure out how to find the time to use them all!

Ultimately, all that "stuff" was sold off after the global financial crisis forced every business to cut costs just to survive, but we often joke about the past and the mental burden that came with having (and finding the time to use) all of those toys.

Nowadays, my dad is enjoying more success than ever but hardly owns anything. He's eliminated all of that stuff from his life, and as a result, he enjoys far more time freedom than he did before. He is less burdened mentally. He is happier and certainly more time rich.

Quite often, when someone increases their income or comes into money, they soon burden themselves with a lot of nice things. On the one hand, they are trying to *look* rich, but, on the other hand, they mistakenly believe that they have to *own* a thing in order to *experience* a thing. A big house loaded with prestige cars and other fancy toys certainly elevates their social status. For others, it's retail therapy or the yearning to live a more adventurous life. But in the long run, once the initial excitement and dopamine hit have worn off, these "things" clutter up their lives with ongoing expenses, endless decisions, and a sense of guilt if they are not used often enough.

After seeing my dad's time and peace of mind robbed from owning too much "stuff," I have made a solemn attempt (in alignment with my definite purpose) not to accumulate things that require more decisions, more money, or more time to run.

Alisha and I have crafted a work-from-home business life that negates needing more than one car. We rent our apartment on the water here to negate having to administer the mortgage, worry about interest rates, pay body corporate fees, maintain and renovate our home, or pay the special levy that was just raised last week. We have investments to grow wealth that is not tied to our emotional needs or wants.

We don't own boats (but do enjoy renting them), don't own a holiday home (but do travel most months to some of the best hotels in the world), don't own office suites, never have to commute, and certainly don't say yes to owning stuff that we know will burden us with even more decisions and administrative tasks. Our burdens are light. We've found that simple scales and complex fails.

To be time rich, you must learn that it's better to experience stuff without obligation than to own stuff that commands it.

But, of course, it wasn't always this way.

Back in 2009, when I was about 25 years old, I got my first bonus check from work, and I couldn't wait to spend it on *something*. A rush of dopamine filled me as I envisioned what it would be like to have a motorcycle again. I had grown up racing dirt bikes when I was young and had fond memories of riding on the back of Dad's Harley as a kid, so I had every reason (in my mind) to want a new Harley.

Naturally, due to my goal of becoming financially independent, I had trouble justifying the purchase. Then I read a book called *A Short History of Nearly Everything* by Bill Bryson, where he talks about how we could be hit by an asteroid at any moment and, despite NASA and the experts scanning the sky, we probably won't even see it coming.

I remember telling myself, *Well, heck, we could be wiped out at any moment, so I may as well splurge on the bike (you only live once)*. That was all the justification I needed. I went out and bought myself a Harley-Davidson Nightster 1200 for about $30,000.

Later, I recall riding it back home from Abu Dhabi one night after a post-work function. It was a 90-minute ride in the dark, and on this particular evening there happened to be a sandstorm (perfect). If you've ever ridden a motorbike in the rain, you know how much it can sting your face. But in a sandstorm, let me tell you, it's brutal. By the time I got back to Dubai, my eyes felt like they were bleeding!

The purchase had been fun, adding parts was fun, and riding it each Saturday was okay. I even joined a local club, but eventually, the novelty wore off.

I later repatriated the bike to Australia, which required a ton of money and paperwork. But due to endless weekend rain, it mostly just sat in our basement gathering dust. It wasn't practical for everyday riding, but I knew if I let it sit there too long, the tires and battery would go flat. More than that, I felt guilty not using it, like I was neglecting a family member.

Finally, on my thirtieth birthday, I sold the bike and invested the cash into shares. I haven't owned a motorcycle since—a decision that has spared me from a lot of further decisions, guilt, and expenses. Occasionally I get a "rush of blood," as my dad calls it, and feel the need to buy another bike, or Ferrari . . . or even occasionally a property! But I fend off the initial dopamine hit by thinking forward, pretending like I already own it, and imagining what further decisions and mind clutter would emerge after the novelty faded.

Instead of buying fancy new stuff, I look for ways to have experiences. This helps me to avoid piling up my day with the decisions and "decision fatigue" that comes from ownership.

Time-Rich Mindset: Wealth = Freedom of Time

Real wealth comes from having freedom of time, not from owning things. That's the time-rich paradigm. The only things I really own these days are assets that generate income. Even then, I invest in assets that don't require a lot of decision making from me.

I prefer investing in stocks to investing in real estate. There are plenty of financial gurus who will tell you to purchase rental properties so you can enjoy passive income. But I know if I invested in property, I would have to make decisions about tenancy, renewals, property management, insurance rates, upkeep, selling, accounting, and more. In fact, in my opinion, owning rental property is a nightmare even if it generates some passive income. I want fewer decisions in my life, not more, so I own assets that produce income and grow in value for me without taking more of my time.

True wealth is synonymous with the liberation of time. Imprint this notion deeply in your mind. It is far better to have extra time on your hands and more money in your pocket than extra stuff in your garage. Stuff demands decisions, and decisions create clutter in your mind, leading to a sense of fatigue and robbing you of your time, money, and attention.

Remember, nothing lives in your head or your garage rent-free, so never organize what you can discard. Remove all of the things that distract you from what you truly love.

Elimination of Stuff Tactics

First tactic: Identify things in your house that you no longer need or use. List them on Facebook Marketplace to sell.
Second tactic: Before making a decision to buy something, list all the subsequent decisions you'll need to make to manage and maintain it.
Third tactic: Buy one fun thing at a time and use it well rather than cluttering your life with multiple fun things.

The Burden of Property

Paul and Tracey, students in our mentorship program, once owned numerous properties filled to the brim with the accumulated "things" they had acquired over the years.

However, on completing our program, they made the decision to sell their properties and part ways with a significant portion of their personal belongings through various sales on Facebook Marketplace.

They then decided to redirect the proceeds into an index fund, ultimately resulting in a multimillion-dollar asset that is now generating substantial passive (and nearly tax-free) income for them. The management of the portfolio is effortlessly handled by a very low-cost fund manager, enabling them to enjoy cash flow without the burden of constant decision making.

Their newfound strategy brought them immense happiness compared to before, when they felt overwhelmed by decision fatigue and the upkeep of possessions. Liberated from an unnecessary amount of stuff, their time and happiness flourished. With flexible schedules, they now relish life more fully, and they are passing on these healthy habits to their young son, ensuring he will be well equipped to forge a time-rich life in the future. They now express their gratitude to me every Christmas and acknowledge the role my encouragement played in transforming their lives.

I hope this story inspires you to do something similar. Think about what things may be stored in your garage that could be sold to kick-start a business or invest in assets to provide perpetual cash flow and free up more time. Could you identify enough items in your garage that could be sold to generate $500? My first million-dollar business began with a modest $500 investment. Surely you could do the same.

Exercise: Sell Your Stuff

How it works:

- Start implementing our first tactic. Identify and take photos of items in your house that you no longer need or use. Chances are you've got junk sitting around that other people would buy. It's packed away in boxes, or collecting dust on shelves, or sitting in your garage. Well, it's not doing you any good now, so start getting it ready to sell.
- Put the items up for sale on Facebook Marketplace. Tools, toys, technology, clothing, collectibles, whatever it may be, use Facebook Marketplace to turn those items into money.
- Take the extra cash and invest it into cash-producing assets or use it as seed money for an income-generating business idea.

If you would like some help implementing the Law of Elimination, head to the back of the book and click the link or scan the QR code to book a free Time Rich coaching session with our team.

Chapter 5

Third Law

The Law of Leverage

"Give me a lever long enough and I shall move the world."
—Archimedes

It is said that when Archimedes was killed by a Roman soldier during the siege of Syracuse in 212 BCE, it set mathematics back 1,000 years. The man was arguably an even more brilliant mathematician and physicist than Newton and Einstein. Among his important works, he is particularly noted for his research on levers, and according to a few early writers, he demonstrated his ability to move incredibly heavy objects simply by using a long enough lever placed on a sturdy fulcrum. What he discovered was the ability to achieve more with less effort, a phenomenon known as *leverage*.

And that brings us to the opening quote of our chapter. If you have enough leverage, you can pretty much move anything. Albert Einstein famously called compound interest the eighth wonder of the world, in which case I would suggest that the ninth wonder of the world is leverage.

Now, I'm not talking about a literal mechanical lever as our old friend Archimedes would have used. Rather, I'm talking about achieving more with less by leveraging people, systems, and capital in order to create time, wealth, and freedom for yourself. Author and coach Dan Martell calls this "buying back your time."

Let's get a bit more specific. When I talk about leverage, I mean three things:

1. **People leverage:** getting people to do the work for you, and compensating them accordingly
2. **Systems leverage:** using software or machinery to automate repetitive work for you

3. **Capital leverage:** deploying capital strategically to generate more capital without using your time (making money while you sleep)

These three things are so important and so central to creating a successful life with all the freedom and flexibility you could ever want that we're going to explore them in some detail over the next few chapters. I want to make absolutely sure that you understand how to do this by the end of the book.

But first, here's an overview of these three types of leverage.

People Leverage

How did the pharaohs of ancient Egypt build the pyramids? Well, they certainly didn't do it all by themselves. Can you imagine if Pharaoh Khufu had behaved like most people, stubbornly refusing to delegate because "if you want something done well, you have to do it yourself"?

Picture old Khufu marching out into the desert of Giza every day and straining to move the giant blocks into place all by himself, working seven days a week without taking any vacations because he had a vision, a goal, and he was determined to get it done. Some of the blocks in the Great Pyramid weigh up to 80 tons. How long do you suppose it would have taken Khufu to complete his vision and reach his goal if he'd tried to do it all by himself?

Well, quite frankly, he *never* would have finished. He never would have come close to creating anything that looked even a little bit like the original plan. But Khufu was no idiot. He didn't try to do all the work by himself. Instead, he used thousands of conscripted workers to build it for him, and, as a result, it was completed in about 27 years. Contrary to popular belief, the people who did the actual construction work of the Great Pyramid were not slaves. Most archaeologists believe they were paid for the work.[1] In other words, it was a job.

You may not be a pharaoh, but the same principle applies. That big, ambitious vision you have in your head for achieving success? You don't have to do all the work by yourself. You can pay skilled people to do the work for you.

Now, people are tricky. If you want them to do good work, then they need to be on board with the mission. They need to have buy-in. Otherwise, they may do less-than-stellar work. They'll call in sick a lot, work less efficiently, and so on. Khufu's workers believed the pharaoh was a living god, so they definitely had buy-in. You probably can't get people to the same level of devotion, but you can certainly get them on board with your vision if you approach it correctly. And, of course, you have to pay people fairly for any work they do.

Here's a small example that even a child could apply.

My five-year-old niece once got some unusual homework from her school. She was tasked with completing household chores, and for each chore she completed, her teacher gave her a gold star. For each gold star she earned, she was rewarded with a dollar. The school's intention was clear: to instill discipline, hard work, and the habit of earning through effort.

However, as I discussed this assignment with my sister-in-law, her mother, a thought crossed my mind. What if, instead of doing all of the chores herself, my niece used a bit of entrepreneurial prowess by paying her younger sister to do some of the work for her? She could teach her sister how to perform the tasks, then pay her 50 cents from each of her dollar earnings. The chores would get done faster, which would bring in gold stars and dollar bills faster, with less time commitment from my niece.

This is a great example of people leverage, and it would have been a win-win outcome for both of the girls. It not only would have served as an ingenious way for my niece to avoid some of the chores, but it would have nurtured her sister's growth. One girl masters the art of delegation, the other gains knowledge, and they both enjoy the financial reward. It's important to keep this in mind so the guilt of getting other people to work doesn't keep you from delegating tasks to others. Delegation is a win–win outcome, not a win–lose outcome.

Whatever your ultimate purpose is and however you envision your future success, you don't have to do all of the hard work to get there. Paying people to do some of the work for you creates mutual benefit, enables you to accomplish more while doing less, and multiplies your available time.

Systems Leverage

Systems govern the universe. We are part of a galactic system, inside of which we are part of a solar system, and on earth, we make up part of an entire ecosystem. Our bodies are run by a nervous system, a circulatory system, and a digestive system.

Moreover, many of the technologies we use each day, such as our iPhones, Google Docs, email, and appliances, are really just systems that we leverage to save ourselves stress, time, energy, and money.

In fact, that's what the acronym SYSTEM stands for: save yourself time, energy, and money. So why do many of us still burden ourselves with stress and waste so much time, energy, and money by not leveraging the many systems available to us?

The answer is that we're still wired to do the heavy lifting ourselves because it makes us feel productive, because it shows others that we work hard, or perhaps we simply distrust computers and fear technology. Many people I talk to seem stuck in 1987, unable to properly wield the power of the internet, ask simple questions on Google, facilitate meetings on Zoom (yes, even after COVID-19), use social media to advertise, plan their day in Google Calendar, or ask ChatGPT to write their job application for them. Heck, some folks still go *in person* to the supermarket to get their groceries. Old habits die hard.

Like most people, I didn't always have a knack for applying systems to various parts of my life to save time, but being in business really helped me to hone this skill and seek ways to achieve more by doing less—not just in business, but in my personal life, too.

When I joined my dad in the property business, we were generating leads through a telemarketing team. Twelve people sat in the office cold-calling phone numbers out of a phone directory. This was, of course, "how it was always done." But soon, through changes in consumer behavior, government regulation, and competition, it stopped working.

Generating leads is the lifeblood of any business, and if that dies, your business dies with it. So, back in 2013, before it became trendy to advertise on social media, we began leveraging a social networking platform to advertise. Thankfully, it worked. The results enabled us to drastically cut staff costs, reduce office space (cutting rental costs), and improve the quality of our prospective clients, leading to more deals. Without a doubt, this one decision to leverage an available system saved the business.

In our network marketing business, we started out in 2014, as most do, by hosting "in-home parties" and having face-to-face meetings. Naturally, this required a tremendous amount of time and effort, and it wasn't very scalable. We were only able to talk to people who lived locally, and building a subscription-based business one customer at a time proved to be near impossible.

Applying the lessons I'd learned in the property business, Alisha and I sought ways to better leverage technology and systems to scale our business. Rather than face-to-face meetings, we started to use Zoom (six years before COVID-19 forced everyone to use it) to meet with more people in less time. Rather than hosting in-home parties, we started hosting online workshops and webinars to make sales. This was much simpler, saved us a ton of time, and was more easily duplicated to our team.

When COVID-19 came along and nearly wiped out the network marketing industry (due to the death of in-person events), our business thrived, and we hit new records, with over 700 new customers joining per month. One decision to leverage technology and systems saved our business and our time.

Despite what you might think, creating leverage through systems and technology is not just for business owners. By applying this newfound knowledge to everyday life, a working single mum can certainly alleviate the pressures of time by delegating tasks to a system. That means groceries home delivered, AI language models to help with administrative tasks at work, YouTube to help with your kids' homework, online dating to get back into the relationship game, social media or apps to create a side hustle income from home, or software such as Upwork to seek work-from-home opportunities to negate a daily commute time and expenses.

Systems, when applied correctly, will automate repetitive tasks and do all of the heavy lifting for you, thereby saving you time, energy, and money. The key is to prioritize setting them up, then let them run while you sleep.

Capital Leverage

People sometimes call in sick, and systems sometimes break down, but money never sleeps, stops, or gets sick. If you put your money to work for you, it will work 24/7. That's how most of the wealth of the last century was generated. It's how the wealthiest people in the world got that way. Warren Buffett became the wealthiest person in the world by deploying capital and leveraging it to create more capital.

Now, I don't want you to misunderstand me. I am *not* suggesting that you should always borrow money to make more money. That's debt (financial) leverage. That's akin to digging a hole so you can fill the hole. Yes, there's a time and place for borrowing, but I'm talking about using your *existing* cash (equity) capital to generate additional wealth. You see, most people spend their capital on the wrong things. They don't use their money in ways that produce more money. They buy sneakers and clothes and cars, but they don't invest in anything they can leverage for future wealth creation.

There's a story about Charlie Munger that illustrates this very well. He had acquired $10 million over time through various business ventures, and he wanted to leverage that capital to create more capital. Charlie was a reader of the financial magazine *Barron's*. In particular, he liked to read the listings of companies that were for sale because he was looking for the right company to invest his money into. He read the magazine month after month for *50 years* but didn't find any companies that piqued his interest.

And then, one day, he came across a blurb about an auto parts supplier called Tenneco Inc. that was being sold cheap. Charlie decided this was it. This was the opportunity he'd been waiting for, so he swung big. He leveraged his $10 million to buy stocks in the company.

Within a year of buying into the company, the stock surged in value, and by the time he sold his position, his $10 million had grown to $80 million. He then gave that $80 million to his protégé, Chinese-born investor Li Lu, who used investing prowess to grow it to *$400 million!*

So, in just two chess moves, Charlie Munger took $10 million he had acquired over the years and turned it into $400 million. That's how powerful capital leverage is. Charlie made two decisions—just two—but they were the right ones. He swung big at the right targets and reaped a huge reward.

This story also illustrates how people leverage and capital leverage go hand in hand because Charlie gave the money to Li Lu and entrusted him with a lot of decisions. Those are two kinds of leverage working together for an even greater result.

Now, each of these types of leverage—people, systems, and capital—has its own nuances. There are ways to use them effectively, so we're going to take them one at a time. In the end, you will understand just exactly how you can use this powerful thing called *leverage* to achieve more by doing less.

Not having enough time is a symptom of not having enough leverage.

> If you would like some help implementing the Law of Leverage, head to the back of the book and click the link or scan the QR code to book a free Time Rich coaching session with our team.

Chapter 6

People Leverage

"When faced with a task, don't ask, 'How can I do this?' Instead ask, 'Who can do it for me?'"

—Dan Sullivan

Over the years, Alisha and I have earned more than 25 free trips around the world as part of the success we've achieved in our network marketing business. In fact, I encourage anyone who wants to travel more without paying for it to build a successful network marketing enterprise for this reason.

On what was our third or fourth trip to Fiji, I was having dinner while sitting next to one of my associates' husbands, who at the time was running a successful lawn care business. He told me he yearned for financial freedom so he could be "off the tools," do more traveling, and spend more time with his family. He told me his business was thriving, but because he did all the work himself, he had no free time. He had reached capacity and could no longer grow his business income.

The solution to his problem seemed fairly simple to me. He could either charge more for his services (meaning fewer clients, more money, and more time) or he could hire someone to do the lawn care for him while he used his additional free time to either win more jobs (scale) or spend more time with his family. He agreed with me in principle, but despite knowing it was true, he said, "Lloyd, I feel like if I hired a worker, I would be burdening someone else with my workload. It wouldn't feel right. Besides, I don't think they would be able to do what I do."

Without realizing it, he was giving me the two most common time-poor mindsets that people exhibit when it comes to delegation. The first is the mistaken belief that when we delegate work to other people, we burden them.

The second is the mistaken belief that "no one can do the job like I can, so I might as well do it myself." I understand both of these ways of thinking because they kept me busy instead of wealthy for most of my working life.

I tried talking to the business owner, but no amount of encouragement could get him to budge. He yearned for freedom, but he was clinging to an old paradigm and, thereby, choosing to remain imprisoned by his old beliefs rather than embracing a new way of thinking. Why does this happen? And, more important, how do we instill a new mindset about leveraging people to win back our time?

Let's take a closer look.

Time-Poor Mindset: Reluctance to Delegate

Our wrong thinking is often a product of ingrained beliefs that developed from things we witnessed growing up. For example, as I shared previously, most of us here in Australia grew up hearing some variation of the saying "If you want something done well, you have to do it yourself." This is such a widespread belief here that most of us assume doing everything yourself is the *only* way to ensure optimal results.

Of course, this idea carries a tacit assumption that your own abilities and prowess surpass everyone else's. That's a rather misguided sense of self-confidence, though, isn't it? To presume that only you can accomplish a task with excellence borders on arrogance. It's an ego-driven notion that comes at a steep cost because when you think that way, you end up toiling endlessly for diminished results.

It's particularly dangerous when it's coupled with the idea that financial success is the result of being busy because it locks people in a self-imposed paradigm that does more harm than good. First, they're convinced that they have to do everything themselves, and second, they fear that if they work less, they will be unproductive. So, they make themselves far busier than they have to be and take on far more work than they should, which robs them of even more time.

Additionally, like the chap with the lawn care business, people are afraid to burden others by giving them work to do. For many, it feels wrong to ask someone to clean your house. It feels wrong to ask someone to fill out paperwork for you. It feels wrong to make them do the "grunt work" of running your life or your business.

But if someone *wants* to do the work, and you're paying them fairly, isn't it a win-win? You're not burdening anybody. On the contrary, you're creating opportunities for them to grow and advance in their chosen profession. And, hey, maybe they'll be better at it than you are, especially if it's their area of expertise.

As we've already said repeatedly throughout this book, doing more work does not necessarily increase your chances of more wealth. It may, in fact, hinder you from focusing on higher-value tasks and diminish your own personal growth and wealth creation. Ironically, being busy may make success much harder to achieve.

As Dan Sullivan puts it, "Results, not effort, is the name of the game. You are rewarded in life by the results you produce, not by the effort and time you put in."

I've seen this play out so many times in the lives of so many people. To break free from this limiting mindset, you have to acknowledge the value of delegation and recognize that true success involves both delegation and collaboration. Success is, and always will be, a team sport. As Alisha often says, "It takes a village."

Time-Rich Mindset: Embrace Delegation

I challenge the notion that hard work defines success. I think the "old money" rich people were onto something. They understood the art of delegation, finding others to do the heavy lifting for them. Ultimately, when it comes to any task, you have a choice: do it yourself or leverage the skills of others. The smart choice should be clear. Only one will provide you with time freedom to enjoy your success.

There's an old story about Henry Ford that illustrates this well. The story comes from Napoleon Hill's classic self-help book *Think and Grow Rich*. According to Hill, during the First World War, a Chicago newspaper called Henry an "ignorant pacifist."[1] Offended, Henry sued the paper for libel. During the trial, defense attorneys tried to prove his ignorance by asking him a wide range of questions on all kinds of topics from American history to science. Henry Ford couldn't answer most of them.

Finally, he grew bored of the questions and said,

> I have a row of electric push-buttons on my desk, and by pushing the right button, I can summon to my aid people who can answer any question I desire to ask concerning the business to which I am devoting

> most of my efforts. Now, will you kindly tell me why I should clutter up my mind with general knowledge, for the purposes of being able to answer questions, when I have people around me who can supply any knowledge I require?[2]

Richard Branson didn't have to become a pilot to start one of the world's largest airlines, Virgin Atlantic. He didn't have to become a rock star in order to grow one of the world's largest record labels, Virgin Records. All he had to do was find people smarter and more skilled than himself to do the work for him.

That's the secret to many legendary wealth and success stories. They are about smart people surrounding themselves with even smarter people and letting the experts do their thing. Ford cracked the code. So did Branson. It appears to be the ultimate life hack for success!

How ridiculous would it have been if Henry Ford had insisted on trying to build every car by hand himself? How silly would it be if Richard Branson believed he had to fly every commercial airplane in his fleet? Yet that's exactly what so many time-poor people are doing. They think they have to do all the work themselves, and with that mindset, they make it practically impossible to grow their wealth.

When I was young, I was a keen athlete. I played basketball, rugby, cricket, soccer, whatever. I remember one day on the soccer field, I ran myself ragged, and finally, I was exhausted. Staggering off the field, I collapsed on the bench and struggled to catch my breath.

The coach turned to me and said, "Lloyd, the reason you're so tired is that you're trying to play every position on the field. If you just stayed in your position, you wouldn't get so tired, and we would probably play better as a team and win the game."

In trying to play all positions, I was achieving less on the field, burning myself out, and hindering my own team's success. That same tendency became a problem for me in business later on. When I worked a nine-to-five job, I didn't have a problem staying in my specific role, but when I left and got into the property business, I began trying to do everything. I was consulting with clients, making sales, conducting inspections, managing staff, and spearheading our strategy. As is the nature of business when you first start, I was wearing as many hats as I could.

Eventually, during a time when we were experiencing a lot of staff turnover in our outbound telemarketing team, I turned to my dad and suggested I roll up my sleeves and start doing the cold-calling myself so we could generate more lead flow.

I remember his response vividly.

"No, mate. Your time is too valuable to be doing that. We will find someone else and better train the team to do it for us." Then he added, "Don't keep a dog and bark yourself." What he meant was "Don't pay someone to perform a task, then do that same task yourself."

The biggest time thief for many people comes from their inability to control the urge to do a job themselves, especially when the job is not being done exactly how they want. I know this urge is hard to control. Every molecule of your body yearns to take back control and do it properly, but you must fight this feeling! Refrain from sliding back into tasks that are well below your hourly rate or skill set.

Why are we like this? Where does this urge come from?

For the most part, old behaviors are just hard to break. If you're used to doing everything yourself, it's hard to let go and hand things to other people. Quite frankly, most of us suck at the art of delegation. Yes, there is an art to it. I knew delegating freed up time to work on tasks that carried more importance and more weight, thereby creating more wealth with the same (or less) effort, but it took me a while to figure out how to do it well. Once I began to master the art of delegation, I was far less inclined to have a dog and bark, too.

To help you to do the same, I've outlined five key steps to follow.

Surrender Control

The first step to successful delegation is to actually surrender the task to someone else, which means relinquishing the control you have over it, including your preferred method of getting it done *and* the outcome. Yes, that means you might watch the person you delegated the task to make a complete mess of it.

There are ways to mitigate this mess, of course, and we will discuss that soon, but first you must be willing to make the leap. Don't be afraid of a little chaos. If you can't relinquish control, how is the other person ever going to develop and learn?

One of my mentors (a master delegator) has a wonderful saying that may help you overcome the old fear of "burdening someone with my work." He often says, "My delegation is your personal development." And he's right. At some point, all of your skills came about because someone else entrusted you with carrying out tasks. Someone gifted you the chance to develop your skills, confidence, and self-belief, so why should you rob others of this same opportunity?

If you refuse to surrender control, you're not just robbing yourself of time; you are also robbing someone else of their personal growth.

Become Strategically Incompetent

Dan Sullivan says, "Delegate everything except genius."[3] These are wise words. But how do you determine your genius, and, more important, how do you avoid doing everything else?

The trick is knowing what you're great at, knowing what you suck at, and being okay with that!

Your genius includes the things you're both good at *and* enjoy doing. For example, Russell Brunson, famed founder of Clickfunnels.com and arguably the greatest marketer to have ever walked the earth, loves (and I mean *loves*) marketing. He lives and breathes marketing, and he's great at it. It's his genius. But when he found himself thrust into the role of CEO at his billion-dollar company, he wound up doing things he was not great at and did not enjoy. So what did he do? He moved himself back onto the marketing team and lived happily ever after.

You see, leveraging people through delegation is not always about delegating *down*. Sometimes, it's about finding out what you truly love to do and outsourcing everything else. How does this relate back to being time rich?

Here's an example.

Have you ever tried to put together Ikea furniture? Talk about a time sink!

Alisha and I bought a chest of drawers from Ikea recently, and it was delivered to us as a flat pack of small pieces with a thick instruction book.

Well, as you now know, "craftsmanship" is at the very bottom of my spiritual gifts (genius) list. Maybe I could become good at it if I tried, but it's not part of my definite purpose, and it doesn't bring me joy. Naturally, it is not a good use of my time (in my eyes), so I have become *strategically incompetent* at it, meaning I know I suck and I am happy to delegate it away to someone else.

Knowing all of this, as soon as I opened the Ikea box, I turned to Alisha and said, "Let's pay someone $70 to build it for us. It'll save us a bunch of time, and the person we hire will probably do a better job than we would anyway."

Alisha (not yet fully embracing my time-rich laws) didn't agree. "This is *our* furniture," she said. "I want to try to put it together myself! It's a challenge, and I'll feel a sense of accomplishment."

Well, I wasn't going to stop her, so I handed her the instruction manual and got out of her way.

She worked for hours putting it together, using the little proprietary tool that Ikea seems to like. In the end, the dresser looked mostly like the picture in the manual, but one of the drawers didn't fit. No matter what she did, she couldn't figure out how to make it fit. Finally, she turned to me, sighed, and said, "Yeah, we should have paid someone to do this."

We both laughed. It was a lesson learned, and now we always outsource unnecessary work, including Ikea furniture, to people who are better at it than we are. It not only helps other people make a living and develop their skills, it also frees up our time to work on more important things and things we love to do that support our definite purpose.

Once you understand both your genius and your strategic incompetence, it becomes a lot easier to know which tasks to do and which to delegate to others. But there's another important consideration.

Determine Your Hourly Rate

It's fairly easy to delegate tasks that you are strategically incompetent at. It becomes more challenging when you have to start delegating tasks you're either good at or enjoy doing (or both). So how do you decide what to do yourself and what to delegate?

Well, one measurable way to approach it is to delegate tasks that are of low value. How do you determine if a task is "low value"? Mathematically, if the hourly cost of doing a task is less than your own hourly rate of income, then delegating it will create more time for you and, at the same time, more money.

The key is knowing your own hourly rate, so let me show you how to calculate it.

To determine your hourly rate, begin with your annual salary and divide it by 52 weeks. Then divide this new number by 20 hours per week (the time typically allocated per week to a side hustle or personal business endeavors). This figure represents your hourly rate.

For example, suppose your yearly income is $100,000. That translates to roughly $1,900 per week. Dividing this weekly income by 20 yields $95 per hour, and that would be your hourly rate. If your hourly rate is $95, then hiring someone to assemble Ikea furniture for $70 an hour makes economic sense. While your delegate is constructing the Ikea furniture, you can spend your freed-up time on tasks that will bring in $95 (or more).

In this scenario, you have still worked an hour, but you gained more wealth from it. Remember, time is wealth, and time is more valuable than money. You must protect it.

You do this by outsourcing tasks that fall below your hourly rate. Make it a habit. This principle, applied in both business and your personal life, allows for prioritization and a focus on what truly matters. It's a strategy for accelerating wealth accumulation while freeing up your time.

(Remember, the simple objective of those who wish to become time rich is to achieve more by doing less—to be less busy and more wealthy.)

I've calculated my hourly rate at about $1,500 per hour. As such, some real-life examples of the kinds of tasks I personally delegate because they are below my hourly rate include the following:

- Building furniture (of course)
- Washing and servicing our car

- Administrative tasks (emails, some social media, email campaigns, design, postage, etc.)
- Advertising, marketing, and sales in our education business
- Writing and developing parts of this very book
- Outreach campaigns
- Accounting and bookkeeping
- Operational management of our brick-and-mortar business
- Booking travel

If you want to delegate economically, so it not only frees up your time but also puts money in your pocket, be aware of your hourly rate and develop a habit of letting go of tasks or projects that fall below that rate. Making this a habit will be difficult at first, but you have to get used to working less so you can earn more.

One of the easiest first steps is to hire a part-time virtual assistant for $8 an hour and start delegating low-hanging administrative tasks to them (www.upwork.com is a great place to do this). You can also hire someone else to clean your house, mow your lawn, deliver your groceries, clean your pool, wash your car, and build your flat packs (www.airtasker.com is a great place to find folks to do this stuff for you). The time liberation will feel exhilarating.

Create Three Lists

The next step in becoming a proficient delegator is to gain absolute clarity about what tasks you're delegating and the reasons behind doing so. Delegating in a structured manner ensures sustainability and progress, so I encourage you to compile three distinct lists. Designate the first list "Can't Do," the second "Shouldn't Do," and the third "Don't Want to Do."

Under "Can't Do," itemize all tasks and obligations in your life that necessitate attention but are beyond your capabilities (your absolute incompetencies).

In the "Shouldn't Do" list, include all routine tasks, such as household cleaning or car washing—all the tasks you could technically handle but would be better off delegating to someone else to save time (tasks that can be delegated at a cost that is below your hourly rate).

Last, in the "Don't Want to Do" list, jot down significant tasks that are crucial but personally unappealing, such as bookkeeping or accounting. These can be your strategic incompetencies, but they might also be strengths that you dislike (e.g., I am great at sales, but I do not love it).

Once you've compiled these three lists, calculate the potential hourly cost for each task if you outsourced it to someone else. For instance, hiring someone to clean your house might cost $30 per hour, while mowing the lawn could be $40 per hour, and administrative work might run at $8 per hour if utilizing a virtual assistant. Sales, however, might be $1,000 per hour (or more).

Bear in mind, you get what you pay for. Don't delegate to the cheapest resource as this may cost you more of your time in constant turnover and retraining. Instead, look for value. What *can* you afford, and what should you *aim* to afford to maintain quality?

Place a check mark beside each item on these three lists that would cost less than your hourly rate to outsource. For each checked item, contemplate the amount of time it would liberate and how you could use that extra time.

THINGS I CAN'T DO	SHOULDN'T DO	DON'T WANT TO DO
1. Build website	1. Emails	1. Sales calls
2.	2.	2.
3.	3.	3.
4.	4.	4.
5.	5.	5.
6.	6.	6.
7.	7.	7.

Do, Document, Delegate

One of the main reasons it took me so long to embrace delegation is that every time I attempted it, I was disappointed by the person I delegated to. My trust in the process faded drastically after a few failed attempts to outsource even the most basic tasks.

Your faith in the delegation process may be at a low point, too, if this has happened to you. Rather than cast blame at the process and say, "Well, it just doesn't work," I recommend taking extreme ownership, like I eventually did. Tell yourself, *I am not that good at hiring and delegating, but I must get better. If others can do it, I can, too.*

This statement will empower you to improve your skills in this important area. Without mastering this skill, it will be nearly impossible for you to become time rich. So how does one become a master delegator?

The first step is to recruit the right person to do the job. If you hire poorly, it won't matter how good you are at delegating; you will get suboptimal results at best. To figure out who is best suited for the work you're outsourcing, you might trial a few people at the same time. It's like not putting all of your eggs in one basket. Request a two-week trial from two or three different service providers and see what kind of results you get. Then you can hire one (long term) based on his or her actual performance and attitude rather than simply hoping and praying that the one person you hire works out. Let the quality of his or her work decide.

Once you have chosen someone from among the three, I recommend a little trick I learned from Codie Sanchez called "do, document, delegate." This framework will help you communicate and train your new resource clearly and mitigate poor standards.

First, **do the task** yourself at least once so you know what is involved (you don't have to be great at it, but you need to be familiar with it). It may not be possible to do this with project-based work, but it works well for smaller tasks.

Second, **document yourself (or someone else) doing the task** by recording video on Loom, Zoom, or your smartphone. This will form the basis of your basic training for your new resource so they can see how you like it done, the quality you expect, and the steps. That way, they can hit the ground running when they start.

For virtual assistant work, I recommend putting your tasks on a Google Sheet that they can tick off daily. Having your tasks or procedures documented and on video also prevents you from training every new recruit if you need to replace them.

Finally, **delegate the task** to the person you've chosen and review their performance. Don't micromanage them. Just sit back and see how they perform. Set up a time to review their tasks each week so you can provide feedback. Ask them if they have any ideas on how to improve your processes.

In the past, I jumped from do to delegate and missed the step in between, which caused confusion and frustration for all parties. Don't skip any of these steps.

As you build trust with your people, you can challenge them with higher-value tasks without necessarily documenting them because they will become more competent over time. However, if they are not doing what you need, see if the problem is a character flaw, a skill shortfall, or poor communication. If it's a character flaw, be fast to fire. Don't keep wasting time and money on people who are unreliable.

As an example, I once recruited an executive assistant who called in sick on her first day of work. It took me 10 seconds to terminate the contract. That's the type of attitude that no amount of training will change. Remember, hire attitude and train skill. You can teach skills, but you can't teach attitude.

People leverage is the most difficult of all three types of leverage because humans are complex and emotional beings, not robots. It's the easiest type of leverage to engage but also the most challenging to manage and scale. There will be a learning curve, but in the long run, it's going to be well worth it.

As Codie Sanchez says, "if you can pay money to steal someone else's 10,000 hours, do it."

> **People Leverage Tactics**
>
> **First tactic:** Begin accepting that you need to surrender control and start identifying those tasks in your life that you're going to be "strategically incompetent" at.
> **Second tactic:** Determine your hourly rate using the formula provided in this chapter.
> **Third tactic:** Create your three lists and determine which tasks in those lists fall under your hourly rate.
> **Fourth tactic:** Begin outsourcing the tasks worth less than your hourly rate, using do, document, delegate.

Escaping the Time Trap

Recently, one of my mentorship students sent me a picture on WhatsApp of a donkey being weighed down with nine enormous bags, and she wrote, "This is me right now. A sacrificial donkey." She wasn't complaining. If anything, she seemed proud of playing the martyr.

I share this not to cast any blame on her because this is what we all do. I used to do it myself. We wear our heavy load like a badge of honor. When I saw the message, I felt sick to my stomach, and I immediately began thinking about who could take some of these heavy tasks off her hands.

The problem is, she's a teacher, and like so many teachers, she feels obligated to do absolutely everything related to her job by herself. This is the attitude of a lot of people in nine-to-five jobs but *especially* teachers. They think, *I have to do all the work because that's what they pay me for!*

But it's simply not true that they can't delegate. She could have easily taken some of her wages and hired someone—maybe a coworker, a friend, or someone on upwork.com or fiverr.com—to take on some of her work, especially the menial tasks that are low value but time-consuming. No matter your job, you can *always* find people to take some of the heavy bags off your back.

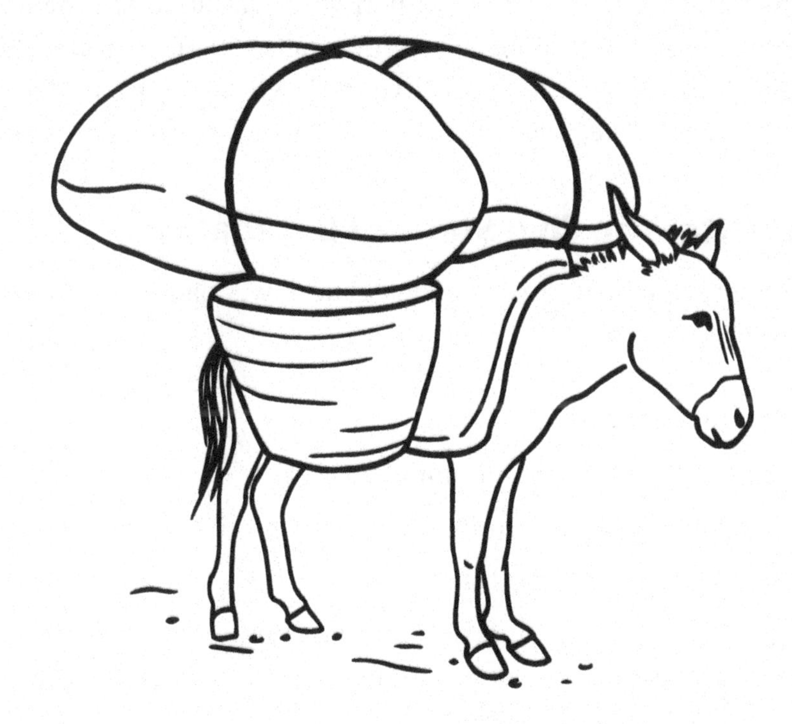

Don't be proud of bearing all of that weight by yourself. You're only hindering your own progress, making it harder to scale your time and wealth, and keeping yourself from enjoying your life. Delegate! Delegate! Delegate!

Another of my students, Christine, is an engineer and a busy mother of four young children. She was developing an app for the National Disability Insurance Scheme in Australia while she was going through our mentorship program, and she was just overwhelmed with all of her responsibilities. Between being a mother, building her business, developing the app, and trying to be project manager for 30 people, she felt like she was spinning out of control.

The first thing I encouraged her to outsource was the cleaning of her house. There was no reason for her to come home from a long day at work and then spend hours doing menial cleaning tasks. This one act of delegation had a profoundly positive effect. Her stress level went down dramatically. That's the power of delegation.

Exercise: The Five Steps of Delegation

Complete the five steps of delegation we discussed in this chapter:

1. Surrender control.
2. Identify strategic incompetence.
3. Calculate your hourly rate.
4. Create your three lists.
5. Do, document, and delegate just one task or job so that you can make the paradigm shift and break the pattern of "doing it all yourself."

Chapter 7

Partnerships

"I can do things you cannot, you can do things I cannot; together we can do great things."

—Mother Teresa

We talked a lot about the power and importance of delegation in Chapter 6, but there's another approach to people leverage that we haven't covered yet. Consider this an important addendum to the previous chapter because the tactic I'm going to share with you now is one of the greatest time hacks of all time.

This one approach enabled me to drastically scale my time while also scaling my wealth. What is it? In a word, *partnerships*.

The partnership method is such a potent method of leverage that I refer to it as *time alchemy*. It creates time and wealth seemingly out of thin air, and it is the reason why I am able to successfully run four separate, profitable companies from the comfort of my wardrobe office.

Across those enterprises, we have one amazing assistant, who lives in Manila. The rest of our teams work independently of us, meaning we keep a very lean two-person team here at the head office (wardrobe): Alisha and me.

How is it possible to run multiple businesses from a small space in our home with only a two-person team on-site? Through partnerships. Dan Sullivan taught me to ask "who" not "how" when it comes to solving problems, but I've taken this principle one step further and tried to find the "who for the who." By that I mean someone I partner with so I don't have to personally recruit and assemble marketing teams, sales teams, manufacturing teams, distribution teams, event teams, and facilities management teams to build our various businesses that span e-commerce, education, events, public equities, and brick and mortar.

The question I ask is, "Whom can I engage to build each of these key teams and systems for me across our many businesses so that we can remain a two-person team at head office?" That's the "who for the who."

Let me share how we've done this across five businesses so you can hopefully learn to do the same—drastically scaling your time and money just as we have.

First Partner: Doing What We Do Best

As I mentioned previously, Alisha and I have been successfully marketing health supplements for about 10 years. What most people don't know is that we do not manufacture, manage supply, or ship any of the products. We don't handle the branding or pricing strategy, and we don't deal with returns and customer service. Heck, we don't even manage the technology or the financial accounts!

It's a collaborative business partnership, meaning we partnered with a North American company based in Arizona that handles all of this for us! Why would we want to take on all those painful parts of business plus take on all of that financial risk? Well, we didn't. So what's the catch?

The company needed help with the distribution or marketing of their products, so we formed a partnership that enables them to do what they do best (back office business management, product development, technology, financials, and operations) and us to do what we do best (front office marketing, sales, and field training). It has been, and continues to be, one of the most fruitful, fulfilling, and profitable partnerships we've ever experienced. They have what we need, and we have what they need—which means we get all of the benefits of a business without most of the headaches that come with running one. It's a highly leveraged business model that has enabled us to scale our income without robbing all of our time. Plus we get to stick to our two-person team here at the head office (a.k.a. the wardrobe at home).

Our sales are made all over the world by 17,000 customers using a simple app and our roughly 75 field consultants who help us market and distribute products and operate from wherever they are in the world by working from their phones. In 10 years, not a single customer has missed a product delivery, and not a single week has gone by when our partner company has not paid us. Not bad for a business that pays weekly, with margins in excess of 25 percent, all without us taking on any financial leverage or risk.

The initial cost of starting this partnership? Just $500.

When it comes to business, you either build businesses or buy them.

In this case, we had to build the business using "sweat equity" (elbow grease), which is why it was so affordable to begin with. Be that as it may, we consciously reinvested a large percentage of our profits into growing the business. The beauty of this collaborative (and highly leveraged) business model is that we could run it part-time while still in our jobs. That's why we were able to reinvest a large percentage of profits (primarily into our own skill development) and scale it to six figures in a little over three years, whereas most others in the same industry were using their profits to pay for lifestyle upgrades.

This business model is accessible to almost anyone. The reason why most folks don't leverage it is because it involves having to learn and implement marketing, sales, and team leadership—skills few folks have the courage or patience to build.

Second Partner: A Perfect Mix of Ingredients

Our financial education and coaching company was formed in a similar way. I had specialized knowledge, skills, and proven results in the areas of money, business, and investing, but I didn't have a clue how to deliver my expertise and "unfair advantages" to others online (at scale).

I definitely didn't want to spend time or energy building my own sales funnels, filming course content, running my own Facebook ads, or writing email copy (among many other things I didn't have the skills or time for), but I was interested in building an education and coaching business.

So, I formed a partnership with my now business partner Jay, who brought all the things that I wanted (time, energy, skills), and I brought the things he wanted (knowledge, money, and network)—the perfect mix of ingredients for a dream collaboration. So, with nothing more than a handshake agreement made in the back of an industrial-area café, Jay and I formed a great win-win partnership where we would start and scale a profitable online education and coaching business together and share in the profits.

Jay became the "who" who assembled a team of "whos" to carry out the marketing work of our education business, and once we solved that problem, another one emerged. We became so overwhelmed with book purchases and prospective coaching enquiries that I could no longer handle the sales calls myself. I had become the proverbial bottleneck in the business. The growth of the business hit a ceiling, which meant every time I traveled, sales would drastically fall. I needed to find the next "who" to replace me, which led me to create the next successful partnership ....

Third Partner: Replacing Myself

As soon as I felt my time being robbed by being "on the tools" (doing all the sales calls myself), I took the uncomfortable steps to replace myself. *What if they don't make any sales?* I thought. *They may not be as good as me*, my ego would say. These are the discussions you will have with yourself the moment before you delegate your work to someone else. I had been let down in the past when delegating, so I was naturally very nervous to let go of this crucial part of the business—although I knew if I didn't, then the business would not scale and I would be stuck on "the tools" making sales calls from home forever. My time was more valuable to me than the money, so I knew in my heart I had to find a solution.

Thankfully, a longtime friend and business associate had been working with a team who could help. While I was sucking my thumb, deliberating whether to engage them or not, that same friend shot me a text and said, "Hey, mate, just made two sales while at my friend's birthday." The penny dropped. It was time to relinquish control.

However, we didn't do what Dan Sullivan suggests by finding a "who" to take over sales for me. Instead, we engaged a *partner* to handle finding and managing the "who" for us.

The team my friend referred me to brought with them all the things I wanted (skills, time, energy), and I brought all the things they wanted (network, money)—the perfect ingredients for a successful collaboration. This was music to my ears because it meant I didn't have to recruit, train, or manage sales team members myself. Again, I could keep our team here at head office (a.k.a. the wardrobe at home) limited to just the two of us.

I still remember the week we transitioned over to the new sales team. It was the same week that friends of ours invited us to spend a week on their yacht sailing around the Sea of Cortez following a few days together in Cabo, Mexico. As we sailed out of the La Paz harbor, without warning we lost all cell and internet coverage and were unable to connect to anyone for the next six days! Talk about bad timing. However, the Law of Leverage was about to prove to me just how powerful it really is.

As you can imagine, I was anxious to get back to phone reception to see if my assistant, our marketing team, and our new sales team had been able to function without me for so long. As we finally sailed back to where we'd first embarked (six days later), my phone started pinging. I held it up to the sky in a desperate attempt to obtain full coverage, and just as I did that, I received a notification from our Stripe account that we had made our first major sale—without me. At the same time, our various books, courses, and content had hummed along with zero involvement from me.

It was an exhilarating experience and another win on my mission to become time rich. As I write this, I'm pleased to say that these two partnerships have helped us build a world-class education and coaching business that is now a Two Comma Club award-winning business—all in just two years from a standing start. It has been a dream team collaboration.

With these partnerships in place, I only had two relationships to nurture instead of 11 (that's the size of our education business team), so I could focus my attention on what I do best: coaching, mentoring, and delivering results to clients. Moreover, it freed up my time to work less *in* the business and more *on* the business, developing our next two partnerships. Alisha likes to say, "We delegate the small deals to free up time to focus on the big deals."

Fourth Partner: Getting into the "Luck Stream"

Our next business partnership came about as a result of the success of our previous partnerships. This is fairly typical in the world of entrepreneurship, where success in one area of a business often leads to (or opens up) the next opportunity. One of my dad's friends, Joe (who once sold a hundred insurance policies face-to-face in a single week with my dad in the 1980s), calls this "putting yourself in the luck stream." By that, he means the harder you work, the luckier you get. Success in one area places you in a position to secure opportunities that many others don't ever get to see (the luck stream).

Unfortunately, most people are so busy working in the business (i.e., on the tools) that they don't have time to exploit these opportunities or partnerships and continue scaling.

My next business, an events business, is only about 18 months old as of writing this, but I have known this partner for about nine years. So, how did it emerge? Well, when you have an education and coaching business, it's extremely important to have in-person events to foster community and culture, but I did not want to spend time or energy becoming an event expert. So, I formed a partnership with someone who already was.

Of course, every successful partnership must be win-win, or it won't work. On this occasion, my friend Morgan had a vision to create a mindset and money event but needed a "money expert" to make it a success. I wanted to run events myself but didn't have the time, skills, or energy to do it all myself. So, again, on the shake of a hand, we created a whole new business partnership that didn't require me to develop it all on my own, meaning I could maintain our two-person team here at head office (a.k.a. the wardrobe at home).

As I write this, I'm pleased to say that as a result of this partnership, we have run a series of very successful Mind & Money events and last month hosted Tai Lopez at an event in Sydney—a wonderfully successful outcome that started with a conversation and a desire to share resources.

What's interesting is that if we had not achieved success through our very first partnership, I would never have met Morgan. Similarly, if we had not developed a successful education and coaching business, I would not have had the resources or skills to form this particular partnership. In this way, the success of the first two partnerships placed me in the luck stream to take advantage of this new opportunity when it arose.

Fifth Partner: My Money, Your Time

We didn't stop there. The most recent (yet certainly not the least exciting) partnership Alisha and I have created is with a friend of 10 years who is a specialist at facilities management and subscription-based brick-and-mortar businesses.

Much like the other partnerships, this one started with a simple handshake at yet another café up the road from where we live. This friend wanted to get into business himself and asked to meet me to get my opinion on some things. As we chatted, I suggested a business that I had personally been wanting to buy, and although I had the money to buy it, I just didn't have the time or skills to run it.

He shared my enthusiasm for the idea and suggested we go in together, to which I replied, "Listen, mate, I've got the money, but I just don't have the time to run a fourth business, particularly a brick-and-mortar-style business."

He said, "Don't worry about that. I'll look after that part."

With that said, we shook hands and began the process of acquiring the business together. As I write this, I am pleased to say we have incorporated and have just settled on our first acquisition (one of many more, I hope).

My contribution to this win-win partnership was 50 percent of the capital backing (money), financial and legal acumen (skills), and some professional services to help (network). His contribution was facilities management and operations (skills, energy, and time) along with a fellow he knew who was selling the business we wanted (network). The beauty of this, like our other partnerships, is that it once again enabled us to keep our lean two-person team here at head office (a.k.a. the wardrobe at home).

The Final Partner: Warren Buffett

There's a final partnership worth mentioning because it will help you to scale your wealth a lot more simply and effortlessly without making you busier. Now, to be honest, I personally manage our public equities portfolio myself, meaning I allocate our capital (profits from various businesses) to buy pieces of public companies (often referred to as stocks). Our portfolio currently consists of just four positions. I actively manage the portfolio because I love to do so. It is an interest and passion of mine, so it is the one thing I don't really "outsource." However, I probably should, and you certainly can.

Technically, about 25 percent of the portfolio is managed by Warren Buffett (could you think of a better partner to manage your money?). Few people realize this, but anyone can have Warren Buffett manage their money for them simply by buying stocks in his company, Berkshire Hathaway. If you'd done this since 1965, it would have returned you over 4,000,000 percent (no, that's not a typo). These days, on average, it can return about 12–14 percent per year (still extremely good) without you lifting a finger. That's a pretty good win-win partnership, don't you think?

Alternatively, you could partner with a fund manager like Vanguard or BlackRock, where one of their broad-market exchange-traded funds would automatically manage your portfolio for you across five hundred American companies. This has historically brought an average annual return of about 12 percent, at a 0.15 percent management fee. Such funds (which are super simple to invest in) actually perform better than what 90 percent of professional money managers achieve. You can literally sit on your backside and do nothing and still beat 90 percent of the professionals who spend 60 to 70 hours a week working hard. Talk about achieving more by doing less—what a partnership!

So, again, why don't I do this with our entire portfolio? Because I'm an idiot and have a sick love affair with "doing it myself." Don't be like me. Keep your money management and investing simple and effective. Consider partnering with Warren Buffett, Vanguard, or BlackRock. You have the money; they have the time, skills, network, and energy.

Note: Warren Buffett himself outlines in his own last will and testament that he wishes his wife's inheritance money to be managed by Vanguard in their S&P 500 Index Fund. How's that for a hint?

Although the mentioned partnerships have played a crucial role in shaping both our financial prosperity and overall success, this was by no means an exhaustive list. I could provide numerous additional examples where resource sharing and collaboration have enabled me to achieve more with less effort. Another notable example relates to the inception of our podcast. Prior to establishing our own successful show, I capitalized on opportunities to appear as a guest on various other podcasts, primarily to promote my first book.

During one such appearance, the host, Phil, made the suggestion, "Dude, why not create your own show?" I had some initial reservations due to time constraints and a lack of knowledge about podcasting, but Phil recognized the potential and generously offered to spearhead the launch and management of our podcast pro bono.

Recognizing our complementary skill set and resources, I gratefully accepted his proposal. I brought financial resources, skills, and my network of connections, and Phil made up for my lack of time, technical expertise in podcasting, and energy to launch. Thus, the *Money Grows on Trees* podcast was born and continues to thrive to this day, with Phil, now compensated for his efforts, as my valued partner.

Partnership Tactics

First tactic: If you're considering creating an online business to generate reliable income for yourself, consider companies that you can partner with that will provide you with tools, systems, and resources (so you don't have to create them yourself).

Second tactic: Look for people who have complementary skills and expertise to help in areas of your life or business for mutual benefit and make an offer to partner with them.

Third tactic: If you're going to invest in income-generating assets, look for a well-known fund manager who will do much of the heavy lifting for you by managing your portfolio at very low cost.

Getting Kicked Together

Why am I sharing these important strategic partnerships in this book? Because I'm trying to show you firsthand how looking for the "who for the who" through win-win partnerships can help you to drastically increase your productivity without robbing your time—to stop being busy and start getting wealthy.

Do these partnerships take time to cultivate and require work to deliver value? Yes, but the work is more scalable. With the use of partnerships coupled with systems leverage (which we will discuss in Chapter 8), we are able to achieve a substantially greater outcome, have a greater impact, and serve more people, all while using less time.

In addition, partnerships bring other subtle advantages, such as broader networks, shared resources, and a substantial amount of extra brain power for problem-solving. My friend says having a partner is great because when business kicks you in the balls, you both get kicked together. If you're going to suffer, it's nice to have a friend who shares the pain. Similarly, when you win, you win together. I can't tell you how incredible it has been to be in partnership with Alisha (in marriage and in business) for close to 12 years, sharing the challenges, setbacks, accolades, and adventures. Success can be a lonely road, so it's best to be in battle with the right people.

Are there disadvantages to partnerships? There can be. I've seen partnerships implode and wind up in court because one party grew envious of the other and did the wrong thing. The risk is there, especially when you are the only one bringing value to the deal. However, if you select the right partner, and if you're both open, honest, and clear about what you want from it and the value you can contribute to it, a partnership can last a lifetime and compound your wealth and life in ways you could not possibly imagine.

I guess it's a bit like marriage. Make sure you select the right partner from the start, and once you find a great match, commit to it for life. Like a fine wine, the right partnerships get better with age.

As the old saying goes .... "When you're young, never get into business with friends. When you're old, only get into business with friends."

Remember, results are all that matter. You don't get extra points for working harder or putting in more effort. The secret of the wealthy stems from the time-rich Law of Leverage. It's not "How do I work harder to achieve more?" but rather "Whom do I find to work with in order to achieve more by doing less?"

Exercise: How to Create a Partnership

Without a doubt, collaborative partnerships are an incredible way to scale your wealth and time. So, how do you develop them?

Well, as you'll notice from the various examples we discussed, to form an effective partnership, two things must happen simultaneously:

- You must bring specific resources that someone else is seeking.
- They must bring specific resources that you are seeking.

Partnerships will not work if you bring all of the resources and they bring none (or vice versa). The key resources you're looking to share with each other will fall into five categories:

1. Money
2. Time
3. Energy
4. Skills
5. Network

The idea is to partner with someone who has more of the resources you lack (and vice versa).

Here are the three steps to forming a successful partnership:

1. **Go for coffee and pitch your vision** to the prospective partner, highlight the resources you both lack (and need), and then suggest a fair deal (share in profits) based on who brings what to the table. It must make commercial sense, both parties must be equitably incentivized with profits, and both must have "skin in the game" (they must have some level of risk on the table).
2. **Test and measure the business model** and efficacy of the idea before officially formalizing your partnership, meaning, just do some work together and see if the idea has merit. If not, abandon.
3. **Formalize the partnership once profits are realized** and you find each other easy, fun, and enjoyable to work with. Schedule monthly meetings, decide on responsibilities (who is in charge of what), and keep an open and honest dialogue going with each other.

Partnerships, like marriage, are built on trust, not contracts. So long as you maintain trust, your partnership of shared resources, ideas, and companionship will compound your wealth and free up your time in ways you can't imagine. The key to attracting a great strategic partner is to deserve one. Be easy to work with (e.g., don't be difficult), be reliable, and be useful. Greatness attracts greatness. The longer a partnership goes, the more valuable it becomes, and the sooner you embrace the fact that you can't do it all on your own, the sooner you will become time rich.

Chapter 8

Systems Leverage

"SYSTEM = Save Yourself Time, Energy and Money"

—Mark Victor Hansen

As we have said, the entire universe is composed of a series of systems. From the movements of galaxies and solar systems all the way down to the subatomic and quantum level, it's the way the whole cosmos operates. Systems keep things moving in fairly predictable, repeatable patterns that can be scientifically observed.

Things work better in systems than they do in bespoke fashion. First, we create a predictable process (a series of repeatable steps) to make things more efficient, and then we automate parts of the process by leveraging software and machinery. When you automate parts of the process, you free up your time.

That's how the super rich multiply time. Sometimes, it's a "soft" system that guides their actions through an efficient, predictable, repeatable process. Other times, it's a "hard" system (software, apps, or machinery) that physically automates repeatable work, taking it entirely off their plate. Before implementing hard systems in your life to automate tasks, you must first get clear on the soft system or process that will be automated.

Let's take a look at a famous example of this in action.

The movie *The Founder* portrays Ray Kroc, former CEO of McDonald's, in a decidedly negative light, and I'm not here to try to restore his public image. However, his story does provide us with a pretty good example of leveraging a system to create success.

The McDonald brothers were running a single hamburger stand in San Bernardino, California, in the 1950s. They'd come up with a process of food preparation that was fast and efficient.

They'd even sold the process to a few other restaurants, but they didn't have a vision for leveraging the system themselves in a large-scale way.

When milkshake mixer salesman Ray Kroc stopped by their restaurant in 1954, he saw how their process could be systematized across countless locations. So, he made a deal with the McDonald brothers and began building restaurant locations all across the country, and eventually all over the world. Along the way, he transformed the company's process into highly repeatable systems that were so simple and routine that even teenagers could operate the store. But most important, because it was so well systematized, it could be duplicated across any location anywhere in the world.

The McDonald's process leveraged people, of course, but also technology to make the whole process of ordering, cooking, preparing, and serving food more efficient than it had ever been, and it ultimately reshaped the entire food industry. Customers loved it because it saved them time. They got the food in their hands faster than ever before. And whatever you personally think about McDonald's food, its massive global success is undeniable.

In the book *The E-Myth Revisited*, Michael Gerber says,

> Pretend that the business you own—or want to own—is the prototype, or will be the prototype, for 5,000 more just like it. That your business is going to serve as the model for 5,000 more just like it. Not almost like it, but just like it. Perfect replicates. Clones.[1]

The reason for this? Because it is difficult (perhaps even impossible) to scale and systematize things that are done differently every single time. You can essentially only systematize things (to save time) when the inputs are predictable and, therefore, repeatable. This is how Ray Kroc scaled McDonald's, and this is the same approach I encourage you to take in order to scale your time.

It's important to recognize that this principle doesn't just apply to business. In almost any area of your life, you can leverage systems to take a lot of repeatable tasks off your hands, make them far more efficient, and free up your time to pursue more important things.

Soft Systems Versus Hard Systems

When we talk about using systems, we're not just talking about apps and software. There are also so-called soft systems that take work and transform it into predictable and efficient steps. The process first invented by the McDonald brothers is a perfect example of a soft system. They created easy, efficient, repeatable steps for taking orders, preparing the food, delivering the food, advertising, managing the store, training the staff, and selling the franchises. When all steps are systematized, they become much easier to duplicate, automate, and scale—saving incredible amounts of time.

I recently watched a YouTube clip of a nine-figure solar panel entrepreneur who joked with the interviewer that even people's bathroom habits are systemized.

Now, you don't have to go to those same lengths in your own life or business, but you can use soft systems to speed up your productivity in many areas by developing step-by-step processes that are more efficient, predictable, and repeatable. For example, you may "theme" your days in your diary to prevent yourself from wearing too many hats on the same day. You may design a more effective morning routine that has predictable, repeatable steps so you save time by not having to think about what to do next. Heck, I knew a guy who arranged his keys on his key chain in order to save time unlocking his front door.

Soft systems aim to streamline tasks by reducing the number of decisions needed, thereby getting you to the end result faster. Success here means reducing decisions, minimizing steps, batching various errands, and even arranging your days, mornings, and tasks with more predictability. For example, if you're going to clean your house every Saturday, you'll get it done a lot faster if you create a step-by-step process or checklist that directs your cleaning in the most efficient way possible rather than just "winging it" every time. Notice how much faster you get the shopping done, and even save more money, when you have a concise shopping list instead of browsing the aisles?

When you have a repeatable process in place, it saves time because you know exactly what comes next. Soft systems and hard systems work very well together. Develop a soft system first to make work more efficient, and then apply hard systems to do the repeatable work.

This is exactly what we do in our various businesses. After all, isn't a business simply a series of repeatable steps that predictably deliver value to people in exchange for profit?

In all of our businesses, we have a predictable way of finding prospective buyers, making sales to them in a repeatable, predictable manner, and delivering value to them in a repeatable and predictable way to help them solve their problems. That's how we earn predictable and repeatable profits.

If we were to change our approach every single time someone asked for help, we would have unpredictable inputs, and as a result, we would get unpredictable outputs. Our profits would not be consistent or predictable, and we would not be able to apply sufficient apps or software to each step to speed up the process. That's why a soft system must always precede a hard system.

In life and in business, the more consistent your steps are, the more likely it is that you will be able to apply software and automate various parts of the process.

Don't be afraid to discover what's out there. Even if you're not tech-savvy, start testing some of these systems out and see how well they work for you. Success loves speed, but that doesn't mean you have to work more furiously. You can leverage systems to do the heavy lifting.

Imagine enjoying repeatable income every week that is being generated by systems that require almost no management. It's possible. I know because I've done it.

When we built our network marketing business, we didn't have to do all the grunt work ourselves because we could leverage hard systems that were already in place. The technology, apps, and websites for ordering, shipping, and payment systems had already been developed by the company. All we had to do was leverage them. That's how we created a repeatable income of $200,000 per year.

Beyond the tech, we also created a soft system in our step-by-step marketing and selling process that was repeatable and predictable. As we brought more people on board, it was easy to train them to use the tech and follow our proven and repeatable steps to produce the predictable results they were seeking, which led to consistent profits.

Even before I got into the network marketing business, back when I was working in the property business, I looked to systematize things more efficiently. For example, we had a group of telemarketers calling prospects from our office. However, it was a slow and laborious process because they were manually dialing numbers from printed sheets of prospect lists. We needed to speed up this process somehow, so we finally implemented an automatic dialing system.

It might seem like a small change, but after we adopted the system, we went from 1,000 calls a day to 18,000 calls a day. Think about it: Our productivity increased by 18× simply by automating the dialing of phone numbers! Although this didn't increase our income by 18×, it did enable us to achieve far more with the same input of time.

Since then, I have constantly looked for ways to use technology to enhance productivity, reduce the workload, or leave the workload the same but drastically increase the outcome.

My podcast also leverages a hard system. I create the content, and then technology constantly delivers it to my audience. Right now, as I work on this book, I am delivering value to customers all over the world who are downloading and listening to my *Money Grows on Trees* podcast episodes via the Spotify app. My work is already done, but the technology allows my message to be played 24/7. My podcast episodes tend to get thousands of downloads each. Can you imagine if I had to personally reach out to each one of those people to deliver the lessons to them? I'd be dead.

Social media is another hard system that enables me to efficiently communicate with a larger audience in less time. Think about how much social media has changed the business game. A few decades ago, salespeople had to walk from door to door and try to make sales individually to one person at a time for one product at a time. My father worked in life insurance, and he spent countless hours driving across the country to meet clients face-to-face. He had no sophisticated systems to streamline the sales process for him. It was entirely reliant on direct personal interactions.

And now, in our current era, I marvel at the opportunities provided by social media for reaching people globally from the comfort of my couch. I can easily "door knock" in my undies from the comfort of my bed if I so choose. That's how far we've come, thanks to technology.

Time-Poor Mindset: Technophobia

Yes, indeed, technology has provided us with more options than ever for automating processes, but many people hesitate to take full advantage of available systems. They may not realize all of the systems that are available to them, but even if they do, many folks are reluctant to learn and implement the time-saving features of a new app or software. They wrongly assume they need some special knowledge or expertise.

People suffering from technophobia will often say things like "I'm not a tech person." They mistakenly believe that software, apps, and other systems are only for the tech-savvy, when in reality, the truly smart, tech-savvy people develop and design these incredible systems for dummies like us! Besides, you can usually find a walk-through for any app or piece of software on YouTube. The only problem is that most people are not looking for answers to their problems on YouTube.

This kind of technophobic thinking keeps most people time poor. In truth, there are a ton of software applications today that are user-friendly, simple, and incredibly effective at carrying out repeatable tasks for you so you don't have to, and unlike leveraging people, they don't require any management. Systems don't sleep, don't call in sick (often!) and can work while you're doing something else. Objectively, those who can make simple apps and software work for them become masters of their time.

There's a whole world of apps and software that could be making your life easier right now. So, why aren't you using them?

Perhaps you harbor reservations about technology due to a traumatic experience with a printer from 1992, so allow me to address this directly: it is now 2024, and in most cases, technology these days is far more dependable than most people are.

Sure, you may encounter the occasional glitch, but as I said earlier, systems don't succumb to illness, harbor hidden agendas, or experience fatigue. By employing simple yet powerful apps and software in your life, you can leverage them to your advantage, confident that they'll continue functioning even when you're asleep or otherwise preoccupied. Have you ever wanted to clone yourself? This is how you do it. Rather than being in two places at once, imagine being in 50 places at once.

So, much of the work you're doing right now could be handled by creating repeatable processes in apps and software. There's no reason for you to keep doing it. Even if being busy makes you feel good about yourself, you're limiting your ability to free up your time for more important things.

I'll never understand why some people boast about how many hours they work in a week. "Oh, man, I just worked 70 hours," they'll say with a big grin, as if they have accomplished something admirable. When you finally start using systems to do a lot of your grunt work, you may feel weirdly guilty, as if you're somehow cheating. And I suppose that's exactly what you'll be doing: cheating time. But that's a very good thing because it unlocks your potential to create a much better life for yourself and your family.

Time-Rich Mindset: Working Smarter

You've probably heard the saying "Work smarter, not harder" a million times, but how does one actually do that? You'll be happy to know it's relatively simple. You look for leverage. You find a "who" (person) or a "what" (system) to do it for you.

The key is to start small. You'll be shocked as to how many simple apps there are that can do the heavy lifting for you. Once you learn how to use them properly and get into a routine of using them, you'll reduce decision fatigue and free up a lot of time.

What will you do with the extra time you create? The answer is "whatever you like," but to move your wealth to the next level, I'd encourage you to spend it on tasks that command higher skills and result in higher profits. With that in mind, let's look at some of the basic systems that you should be using (at the very least) to streamline and automate various tasks in your life to achieve more by doing less.

Google (www.google.com)

Let's start with the simplest, yet one that is still vastly underused by most people. Back in the day, if you wanted to settle a dispute with a friend at the pub as to who won the 1991 Melbourne Cup, you had to go home, open your 26-volume *Encyclopaedia Britannica*, pull out the right volume, and flip through pages to find the topic you wanted to learn about. Even then, not all answers were readily available or even up-to-date. Finding answers was hard.

Now all you have to do is pull out your smartphone, open the Google app, and ask your question. Within seconds, Google will give you links to far more relevant information than the *Encyclopaedia Britannica* could ever provide. A whole world of knowledge is in your pocket—or in your purse, or possibly in your hands—at this very moment.

Even though Google was launched on September 4, 1998 (more than 26 years ago), most people still fail to take full advantage of this simple software. In my daily interactions as a coach and mentor, I find myself fielding questions from students even though the answers are readily available on Google.

For me, Google has become a go-to resource whenever I want to know something quickly. There's no reason to stay in the dark about any topic. I can pull out my phone and find information and answers almost instantly. Let's suppose I want to talk to students on the other side of the world. Instead of trying to calculate what time it is in their location, I can simply ask Google "If it's 10:00 a.m. in Brisbane, what time is it in Las Vegas?" and I will get an immediate and accurate result (4:00 p.m., by the way). Yet I can't tell you how many people still struggle with simple time zones.

The time saved by harnessing Google's capabilities is substantial, and it has enabled me to deal with the intricacies of global communication, information, and guidance with efficiency and ease. Remember, your brain is for creating ideas, not storing information. If you're not delegating your questions to Google's search capabilities right now, you are working too hard and most probably losing time.

YouTube (www.youtube.com)

YouTube has also been around for a very long time, and I am shocked as to how little people use it. I have a buddy who recently sold his business for $50 million, and he once said to me that he would just about fire anyone who came to him with questions that could be easily found by watching a few YouTube clips or searching Google.

I have often joked with some of my students, when they ask a simple question, by responding facetiously, "It must be your lucky day. I have just been granted access to the most incredible video library that answers almost any how-to question on earth at the click of a button. It's truly incredible. Would you like the link to access it?" They lean in with excitement, ready for it, and laugh when I send them the www.youtube .com link.

As a mentor, my job is to develop independent leaders and thinkers who can self-motivate and self-solve their own problems—not to provide answers to basic questions that can be readily found using simple software. What's fascinating is that *all* of the basic software and apps I'm discussing here can be learned and applied by asking YouTube to teach you. In fact, I'll go so far as to say you could learn the entirety of grade school and university, all on YouTube...for *free*. Where do you think I learn most things? Books and YouTube. Stop waiting for someone to spoon-feed you answers on tech, travel, and world facts. Start delegating your needs to YouTube and save yourself time, energy, and money.

Social Media (Let's Call It Meta)

This has also been available to the general public since 2006, and yet it amazes me how underused it still is in 2025. It is a powerhouse system for building connections, creating communities, searching, selling unwanted stuff, and, most important, advertising your business or personal brand (globally) at little or no cost.

It's arguably the greatest tool for making money that has ever existed (aside from Apple's iPhone), which is why I am in shock when people tell me they don't use it yet wish to grow their wealth, grow their business, and grow their network and opportunities.

Nearly all of our businesses were scaled using social media. Why? Due to its incredible leverage: 98.5 percent of seven-figure businesses use paid social media advertising. It is the most potent advertising vehicle to ever exist. Never before have you been able to locate your ideal client or customer (at scale) with such little effort. Even my dad's 30-year-old property business harnesses the power of inbound lead generation all from Facebook. It's imperative, if you are wishing to achieve more with less and create more opportunities for yourself, that you start to better leverage Facebook, Instagram, LinkedIn, X, or TikTok.

But it's not just for those wanting to scale their business.

Social media is like a business card on steroids. It is the shop front to your virtual shop. It is your *live* résumé. It is your personal brand. It is your gateway to the world. If you're an employee and don't think you need social media, you're dead wrong. Building a profile and personal brand using basic, organic social media marketing can substantially enhance your chance of finding a better job, finding a new job if you lose the one you have, connecting with a potential life partner, and/or staying up-to-date with the world.

Social media is no longer just for teenage girls to chat (maybe Myspace was back in 2004). It is the ultimate system to create more leverage in your life. Don't be a dinosaur—start learning it now.

Zoom (www.zoom.com)

In the early days of my online businesses, I used to hit the road often for in-home presentations, face-to-face events, and coffee meetups with potential clients, and back then one of the few ways to present to a group was by hiring a local venue. It was costly, time-consuming, and downright draining. Then, about nine years ago, I embraced Zoom, recognizing the potential it gave me to connect with people, present, and run events from the comfort of my own home. Fast-forward to the COVID-19, and suddenly everyone was on Zoom, catapulting us all into the twenty-first century. It revolutionized business and productivity globally.

Nowadays, instead of hopping over for a coffee, I'll get on a quick Zoom call and save a ton of time and money. This shift in approach is why I can effectively manage multiple seven-figure companies and a substantial investment portfolio right from our head office (yes, my wardrobe). But to really leverage its power, you will have to move from Zoom "user" to Zoom "producer." Leverage it for meetings for sure, but also learn to use it to run master classes and workshops and deliver group training sessions and video recordings for content production or documenting to your team for training modules.

Recently, my accountant and I did our books all over Zoom, when before it would have required a meeting in his office. Heck, Alisha used it to run fitness classes from our lounge room during COVID-19. The lesson here is to replace as many of your needs with Zoom as possible. Doing this will save you countless hours. I know for most of you, you will already be leveraging it. But are you leveraging its full power? For those who are still afraid of it ... time to put the big-kid pants on.

Google Calendar (calendar.google.com)

My Google Calendar is like my command center for managing my day. We'll talk about this more in Chapter 9, but frankly, this app is the most underused app of them all when it comes to saving and creating more time. If you don't religiously delegate meetings, tasks, deep work, and rest to some sort of digital calendar, you are more than likely suffering from extreme anxiety running basic parts of your life and more than likely very unproductive and unreliable. More on this one later. Download it now.

Calendly (www.calendly.com)

I streamline the scheduling of appointments and reduce decision fatigue using Calendly, which connects to my Google Calendar and enables me (or my assistant) to send a simple link to people to book appointments without causing whiplash with back-and-forth messages. Type into YouTube "How to use Calendly" to learn how it works.

Spotify (www.spotify.com)

Spotify helps me push out content systematically (and for free) through my weekly *Money Grows on Trees* podcast. Although most podcasters have a setup that resembles a NASA launch station, I have a basic RØDE mic that plugs into my iPhone and an app owned by Spotify called Spotify for Podcasters (formerly Anchor) where I can record an episode and directly upload it to my show, across multiple platforms ... for free. That's right, I run an award-winning podcast with over 145 five-star reviews and thousands of subscribers; where people listen to my lessons on money, investing, and entrepreneurship (while I sleep); and we use nothing more than a phone, a mic, and a free app. What's stopping you from doing this?

Download the Spotify for Podcasters app now, grab the RØDE mic from Amazon (online), and start recording your show today.

Canva (www.canva.com)

This is one of the most effective tools you can use to create documents, presentations, creative designs, and content using existing templates. If you are not already using this, then please download it now and jump on YouTube to learn how to use it. If you are a master of leverage, you'll hire someone to use it for you.

ChatGPT (chat.openai.com)

I've saved the best until last. Most recently, I've fallen in love with ChatGPT, the market leader in large language model AI. Without a doubt, this software (or app) may well be the most potent of them all when it comes to you becoming time rich. Why?

Because it is like having a multilingual assistant who can code, advise, calculate, and write just about anything you need, without making errors, calling in sick, taking annual leave, or asking for a pay rise. It is the ultimate answer to systems leverage.

The only other thing that would (or certainly will eventually) come close is Elon Musk's Optimus robot, which they recently developed at Tesla. Seriously, go to YouTube and type in "Optimus robot" and see how advanced this AI learning robot is. It'll be my guess that this robot will soon become the absolute answer to leverage and be present in every household. But until then, we are very lucky to have ChatGPT to fuel our desire to achieve more by doing less—to stop being busy and start getting wealthy.

You can learn to use this incredible software like you can learn anything (via YouTube), but what is difficult is to get into the habit of using it instead of your own effort. I've shown many of my mentorship students how to best leverage it, and many of them are now saving hours and hours per week with this system. It will review and write contracts for you, write emails, sales copy, job resumes, assess investment ideas, diagnose and solve problems, be your therapist, analyze data and much more–all pretty much instantly. Take the time to learn it now. Do not wait for 20 years to go by to catch on to this. It's very simple to sign up with a free account and use it. Add the app, and start by asking it one simple command: "What are the most effective prompts to ask ChatGPT?" Have fun!

Honestly, I could go on and on about all the systems I use. Whenever I catch myself doing a task repeatedly, I immediately start hunting for a system that can automate it. Remember, time is more valuable than money, so if you have to spend some cash to leverage a system that can save you time, energy, and money, do it.

The rich spend money to save time; the poor spend time to save money.

Invest in apps and websites like the ones I've mentioned. Start implementing them to automate all of the repeatable tasks that you do on a routine basis or, better yet, hire a virtual assistant who can use them for you. Finding the "who" (people) to run the "what" (system) is how you truly scale your time and wealth. Double dip into this leverage and you'll be achieving ten times what others achieve, with less effort, too.

And remember, systems change. New systems come along, old systems are supplanted, so it's important to constantly look for new and better ways to automate processes. Don't implement some app and stick with it forever. If a new and better system comes along, be willing to test it and possibly upgrade to remain time rich.

Systems Leverage Tactics

First tactic: Identify the simple, repeatable tasks that you complete on a regular basis (either in your business or in your personal life) and create step-by-step processes or checklists that make them more efficient and easier to repeat. This could include everything from how you clean your house to shopping lists to your sales process to how you set up for industry events to weekly staff meetings.

Second tactic: Start using apps, software, and technology that can take over some of those repeatable processes for you, including the tech mentioned in this chapter (e.g., social media, Google, Calendly, Google Calendar, ChatGPT). For example, you could use your grocery shopping list to schedule regular grocery delivery, taking that task entirely off your plate.

Third tactic: Constantly be on the lookout for newer and better systems. Test them to see if they can make your life even easier.

From Christmas Trees to Clothing

Alton is a student of ours who runs a Christmas tree, landscaping, and storage business. When he decided to ramp up his game, he began using social media for advertising and marketing. As a result, Alton experienced his best year yet in the Christmas tree business, all thanks to the power of leveraging social media.

Then there's Josh and Casey, a dynamic duo who run a sustainable clothing business called Tweedy. When I first spoke to them, they were knee-deep in reactive mode because they lacked consistent systems. A significant portion of their sales came from events and festivals, but they were overwhelmed with the amount of work that went into preparation and setup.

With guidance, they streamlined the setup process for festivals to the point where they could delegate the task to others. This took a whole lot of hard work off their plates.

Beyond event logistics, Josh and Casey took the systematization even further. Their meetings at work now follow a structured pattern, they have implemented online shopping systems to boost e-commerce sales, they have leveraged social media to elevate their brand, and they religiously delegate their emails, letters, and any required writing work to ChatGPT. These strategic systems haven't just increased their income; they've also worked wonders in freeing up Casey's time to focus on what she truly excels at: selling. Similarly, Josh now has the time to steer the ship, develop the business, and lead the teams.

Alton, Josh, and Casey are shining examples of how implementing systems isn't just about boosting income but reclaiming time to excel in the areas where you bring the most value. They've embraced the power of systems, and it is transforming the way they run and grow their businesses.

Exercise: Start Implementing Systems

The exercise for this chapter is simple. I want you to start implementing some systems into your everyday life. To start, I encourage you to do the following:

- Begin getting your groceries delivered. Download an app for a local grocery store and set up regular deliveries. This is going to save you at least a couple of hours a week, and it's also going to save you money. How so? Because when you're not roaming the store aisles, you're less likely to get seduced by cool-looking products you don't need. Most major grocery store chains these days offer grocery delivery. And some of the larger chains, like Walmart, have even begun testing drone deliveries that will fly your order straight to your porch within twenty minutes.
- Next, I want you to download and set up Google Calendar, one of the most underused apps on the planet.
- Start conducting most of your in-person meetings on Zoom. If you have a coffee catch-up meeting with someone this week, try to move it to a Zoom meeting instead.
- Download ChatGPT. Watch some YouTube videos on how to use it, then start testing it for creating your social media posts, marketing content, and whatever else you might need.
- Make sure you have active profiles on Facebook, Instagram, and whatever other relevant social media platforms there are at the time you're reading this. Start posting things and connecting with people. Use Chat GPT to write the posts. Then polish them up a bit and post them.

There are a lot more systems you can implement, but if you start using just the few that I've mentioned here, it will set you on the right path. Get used to off-loading repeatable tasks to hard systems. Start creating soft systems to streamline the tasks you have to do yourself, then either get other people to do those tasks or implement systems.

Embrace the time-rich mindset of getting systems to do most of the work, and see what difference it makes in your life. Then take all of that new free time you've created and focus on higher-value tasks, the things you really enjoy doing, or just use the time to enjoy your life a little more.

Chapter 9

Capital Leverage

"Money's greatest intrinsic value, and this can't be overstated, is its ability to give you control over your time."

—Morgan Housel

When I ask people why they want to be wealthy, the response is usually "I want freedom." Then I ask, "Freedom from what?" Most of the time, they reply, "From my job."

But why do people want to be free from a job? It's simple. Because they want to be able to do *what* they want, *when* they want, with *whom* they want.

The one thing that keeps people trapped in the financial prison of a job is the human tendency to trade time for money instead of trading money for time. In other words, most people value money more than they value their time (Money > Time), but I say wealth stems from placing a greater value on time over money (Time > Money).

Let me elaborate.

Time-Poor Mindset: Spend Time to Make Money

When you value money over time, you're quick to trade your time for some money. This typically happens in a salaried nine-to-five-type job with a capped income or in a sales commission job where your moneymaking is fully dependent on your personal activity. We call this *linear income*, and with linear income, the money you earn is completely attached to your time. You are, in essence, someone else's "people leverage."

This means you can only make more money if you actively give more time. The major problem with this approach is that there are only 24 hours in a day (assuming you never sleep). If you want to chase more money, you will need to sacrifice all of your time to do so, and you will have to keep doing this forever.

That's the cycle you get into when you work hard for money. Your higher income may make you feel and possibly look rich, but income does not equal wealth. In my opinion, real wealth is the ability to exert control over your own time because time (not money) is the true currency of life.

Time-Rich Mindset: Spend Money to Make Time

So, what's the alternative? A quote from Warren Buffett encapsulates a better approach: "The rich invest in time; the poor invest in money."[1]

The alternative approach to scaling your wealth and your time is through capital leverage, a strategy that involves deploying your financial capital to either build or acquire assets that will reliably generate additional income, thereby eliminating the need for you to work and giving you complete control over your time. This type of income is referred to as leveraged income and is completely detached from your time.

By strategically leveraging capital to build or acquire income-generating assets, you can attain a level of financial autonomy where your wealth grows without you having to work hard for it.

Most people aren't doing that. At one time, I wasn't doing that either. Like so many others, I wasn't directing my capital toward strategic investments but rather toward the ceaseless acquisition of material possessions (while accruing more and more debt). I thought this was the path to happiness. However, this approach fails to yield passive income and, as a result, fails to produce more time.

During my time in Abu Dhabi, I was locked in a cycle of increasing credit card debt due to an incessant purchasing of "stuff." I thought the primary purpose of my salary was to spend it on consumer goods, a nice place to rent, and going on more trips, when I should have been using it to buy assets like real estate or stocks in order to generate more income. The path I was on led to a quagmire of debt, emotional turmoil, and assorted problems.

I didn't begin to escape the quagmire until I learned the concept of capital leverage from Robert Kiyosaki and Sharon Lechter's original books, *Rich Dad Poor Dad* and *Cashflow Quadrant*. In the former book, Robert shares his story about amassing enough capital to purchase apartments. Through savvy investments, he managed to generate an impressive annual passive income of $100,000 from rental income.

The most significant personal milestone for Robert happened when he finally attained enough rental income to cover all of his expenses because it was the moment when he finally gained true financial freedom. He no longer needed to work a regular job to pay his bills. All of his financial obligations were covered by passive income. That freed him up to pursue even more lucrative forms of capital leverage, which created more success than he'd ever imagined.

And that right there is the essence of capital leverage: using your financial resources to either build or acquire assets (real estate, businesses, or stocks) that will generate enough income to meet and then exceed your expenses. The end goal is absolute financial freedom, when you simply don't have to work a regular job to afford your current lifestyle.

I actually discussed Robert's journey with the coauthor of the book, Sharon Lechter, on my podcast. During our conversation, she talked about the future that technology is drawing us toward, a time when automation will handle most tasks and a basic universal income will reshape the employment landscape. Indeed, that might be our future, but in the meantime, Sharon strongly urges people to adopt a strategy that will lead to financial freedom.

Drawing on her extensive experience, including serving on the President's Advisory Council on Financial Literacy for two US presidents, Sharon offered a profound piece of advice. When I asked her for her most crucial financial lesson, her response was simple and direct: "You have to buy assets!" Her reasoning was that assets have the ability to generate predictable, repeatable income, freeing you from spending more time to make more money.

This simple yet profound principle is frequently overlooked or misunderstood. People just don't understand how acquiring assets can secure them a reliable income stream and pave the way to true time freedom.

Buy Back Your Time with Assets

Every Monday afternoon, Alisha and I pick up my niece and nephew from school, and they hang out at our place until my sister comes over after work to pick them up. I have been teaching my nephew how to box, and my niece, who's a bit of a soccer superstar, plays *FIFA World Cup* on the Xbox. Recently, we introduced them to the Cashflow board game, which is an interactive experience designed to teach people the path to financial freedom.

The goal of the game, if you haven't played it, is to strategically acquire real estate assets, businesses, or stocks capable of generating enough passive income to exceed your living expenses. Victory is achieved when players attain more passive income per month than their monthly expenses.

The board game is a great tool for financial enlightenment that demonstrates an essential principle of wealth creation: leveraging capital intelligently to create a consistent and predictable income stream, ultimately unlocking the luxury of time.

It works in the game just as it works in real life. First, you acquire income-generating assets. Then you create a system to perpetuate that income and delegate operational aspects to other people or systems (sound familiar?).

This brings together capital leverage, people leverage, and systems leverage in a beautiful way, and it's exactly how Alisha and I created a life of ultimate freedom and flexibility for ourselves.

As we played the game, I told my niece and nephew, "There's nothing we did that you couldn't do yourself, but you have to resist the impulse of instant gratification. Be careful not to spend all of your money on things like cars and holidays, and instead start channeling it toward things that will yield predictable and sustainable returns."

Sharing these lessons with them got me thinking about where Alisha and I first started, entirely dependent on a linear income, and how we leveraged our capital in various ways to eventually generate leveraged income instead.

We began our first business, our network marketing business, with an initial capital injection of just $500, which was possible because we aligned ourselves in partnership with a supplements company that had all the existing hard systems in place.

With a concerted effort and by reinvesting some of the proceeds, we not only made more sales but also trained a team of roughly 75 consultants to become representatives selling on our behalf. The supplements company handled the systems and provided us with a streamlined operation that now generates predictable income on a weekly basis and has done so for over 10 years. Because the products are consumable, many of our fifteen thousand customers across the globe reorder each month. This means we continue to get paid each week even while traveling or working on other projects. Remember, all of this started with a humble initial investment of $500, money I could easily have spent on "stuff."

Our education business also began with a modest capital infusion of $10,000, strategically deployed to engage a partner to create a comprehensive online marketing system to sell our books, online courses, and coaching programs. These elements created a self-sustaining online business that consistently generates income. We then deployed more capital from the profits of the business to outsource the selling process and grow the team so I was free of any sales responsibilities.

Our events business was also started with a relatively small sum of capital. And, more recently, for the acquisition of our newest business, we opted to use the bank's capital to finance the entire purchase!

So, instead of working hard to make money simply to spend it on material things, consider strategically deploying some of your cash to establish a reliable business or investment income stream. There are many different avenues for doing this. You don't need to jump into network marketing or supplements or an online education business if those are not your thing.

You could purchase a franchise, acquire real estate that can be turned into rental properties, invest in stocks, or explore opportunities in e-commerce. As long as you're channeling capital into ventures that enable predictable and repeatable income, then you are leveraging your capital smartly.

Our education business and network marketing business were both meticulously built through an initial capital injection combined with the application of systems leverage and people leverage. At the same time, I've long been following Sharon Lechter's advice by taking a portion of profits from each of our businesses to acquire assets by purchasing stocks in well-established businesses. That's how we created a seven-figure investment portfolio that produces a reliable flow of income to us through various dividend payments.

Each acquisition is a testament to our strategy of leveraging capital to purchase existing assets and enjoying the dual benefits of growing asset values and consistent income in the form of dividends. Every dollar that the portfolio grows or produces in income represents many hours of work we no longer have to do.

When you buy cash-flowing assets, you buy back your time. That's the path to true success with wealth and time freedom:

- Deploy capital to build or buy small businesses that generate (through systems and people) predictable and sustainable income.
- Use a percentage of profits from these existing enterprises to create a profitable, and more passive, investment portfolio (in real estate or shares).

Throughout the years, I've stuck to this approach, diligently setting aside capital from my various business ventures to purchase stocks in existing businesses that will yield income without my constant presence. There are nights when I've gone to sleep and awakened to discover that the value of our portfolio surged overnight by $60,000—a true testament to the power of capital leverage, a mechanism through which wealth grows and income materializes.

Now, many people recommend that you invest in real estate. In fact, Robert Kiyosaki recommends it in *Rich Dad Poor Dad*, but I believe this poses a challenge in today's economic climate. Real estate prices have skyrocketed, making it impractical for many people to enter the market. These days, real estate demands an investment equivalent to 10 times the average earnings, forcing buyers to take on tremendous amounts of debt to make their investment.

For that reason, I prefer investing in stocks as they have a much lower financial barrier to entry and still produce predictable cash flow without the need for drastic levels of debt. It's also less time-consuming, less prone to create decision fatigue, has zero operational costs, and is devoid of the complexities that come from dealing with real estate.

The appeal of this strategy lies in its simplicity. I can leverage my own capital without creating external debts, and I maintain complete control over my investments. No interest payments, no complications. I simply take cash and leverage it to acquire stakes in successful businesses.

This opportunity is open to anyone. Even with modest capital, you can invest in an index fund, which is a collective investment in various companies that provides quarterly dividend payments. It's true passive income. You invest, then you sit back and let the money go to work for you whether you're awake or asleep. Remember, if an investment can't produce consistent cash flow, it cannot produce consistent time. If you invest for capital growth, you'll become asset rich, but if you invest for cash flow, you'll become time rich.

Leverage Your Capital to Build Assets

The true beauty of capital leverage is its versatility—not only does it enable you to create income-generating assets through people and systems, as exemplified by our two online businesses, but it also facilitates the purchase of existing assets, particularly in shares.

This is the essence of the time-rich mindset. Leverage your capital to create reliable money-generating mechanisms and invest in assets. You don't have to have a lot of existing capital to begin this journey. My initial investment, as I said, was just $500.

So, the question you need to ask yourself is, *How can I deploy my current capital to not only produce predictable returns but also foster continuous capital growth?* Believe it or not, you can begin investing and acquiring assets right now through a user-friendly online broker that requires just a brief download and setup process. Even if you only have a small amount of money to invest, you can begin putting it to work for you. You don't have to wait.

I witnessed a remarkable application of capital leverage when a past student of mine shared a story about his fifteen-year-old son. With some wisdom passed down to him from his dad, the teenager started to vigorously save and invest his cash into a simple index fund. As I understand it, the fund is now worth about $60,000 and produces repeatable dividends of $3,000 a year. Imagine what it'll grow to by the time he is 50 years old!

Sadly, a lingering fear of technology and a lack of basic investment education are the biggest hurdles for many people. They simply aren't embracing the opportunities provided by apps and online tools. They're not learning from abundant resources like YouTube and Google because they feel anxious and out of their depth. As a result, they simply don't realize how easy it is to put your money to work to then earn more money.

I can tell you from personal experience that there's a beauty in seeing your own money working tirelessly for you—never resting, never calling in sick, a relentless force operating around the clock.

Start using your capital to buy time. Leverage it to build or buy businesses that will generate repeatable cash flow, and use some of the ensuing profits to acquire additional assets that will yield consistent income. This is how you liberate your time from the constraints of conventional labor.

Using your money to acquire material possessions will only tether you to the typical cycle of working hard to make money. True wealth lies not just in making money but in the liberation of time! Free your time and you will free yourself.

Capital Leverage Tactics

First tactic: Deploy your current capital (savings from your job income) to invest and acquire assets through a user-friendly online broker.

Second tactic: Once you've acquired a bit more capital, build or buy a small business that will generate predictable and sustainable income. Remember, my first business in network marketing only required an initial investment of $500.

Third tactic: Use some of the profit from your new business to create a profitable investment portfolio (in real estate or shares).

Mastering Capital Leverage

When I think of someone who really understands capital leverage, I think of Tyrone, a great man I've been mentoring now for almost two years. When he first joined our program, he felt trapped in his regular nine-to-five job. Sure, it paid well and allowed him to buy real estate and live his life, but he yearned for more.

When he joined our program, he started to allocate more capital to his growing share portfolio (which has now grown sixfold over 18 months) but could see it was still going to take some time to secure the steady passive cash flow required to cover his living expenses and free him from the nine-to-five grind.

Having learned the principles of leveraging capital to buy assets, he made a critical pivot. He decided to sell a property investment he'd made and use the equity capital from the sale to buy a gym franchise. He knew the gym was already a proven business, knew it was already gushing repeatable cash flow, and knew it was arguably a more effective use of his capital than just waiting years for his property investment value and income to rise.

The move worked, and now (through applying all methods of leverage) he not only has the gym business producing income, but remarkably, he's been able to stay in his job and continue to grow his dividend-producing share portfolio. The next phase of his journey will begin very soon when he transitions out of his job and full-time into his business where he will have more time freedom.

In fact, many of our students routinely leverage a small amount of spare capital to build a second income-generating asset (e.g., an online business outside of their current business or job) and consistently invest some of the additional cash flow into other assets, like stocks. This accelerates the growth of their wealth and their cash flow, thereby accelerating their ability to buy back their time.

Exercise: Deploy Some Capital

I'm going to help you get started leveraging capital. Here are your first steps:

1. Open an account with a micro-investing app (Raiz, Acorns, or Moneybox) and put $10 in it.
2. Watch a video on YouTube on how to use the account.
3. Invest that $10 into one of the various index funds they offer.

There you go. You've taken your first step toward leveraging your capital. As you make more money, funnel more of it into the index fund.

You're on your way. See how easy that was?

Chapter 10

The Fourth Law

The Law of Priority

"If you always feel like you don't have enough time in the day, you're probably doing the wrong stuff."

—Alex Hormozi

"As long as I stay busy, I'll make money and get rich." A lot of people think this way. They falsely believe that being busy means being productive, and the busier you are, the better your chances of getting wealthy.

This wrong thinking has trapped a lot of people in a downward spiral of stress and frustration, and sadly, it's just not true. Being busy makes you busy, and that's all it does. On the contrary, if you want to be productive and actually create wealth or time, then you have to avoid busyness, engage leverage, and consciously prioritize high-value tasks that move the wealth and time needle.

Time-Poor Mindset: Reacting to the World

It doesn't matter how hard you work; if you're working on the wrong things, you're wasting valuable time and energy. Not only are you wasting time and energy but also you are hindering yourself from making real progress. Having a daily schedule that is chock-full of urgent tasks, projects, and activities might make you feel productive, but it's a mere facade if they lack importance.

You're going to be stuck on the hamster wheel for the rest of your life until you decide to begin ruthlessly protecting your daily schedule and focusing on tasks that support your definite purpose. The Law of Priority isn't just a matter of prioritizing what you want but, more importantly, getting clear on what you will give up to get what you want.

Most people have to-do lists that are absurdly long and wildly misprioritized, full of things they feel obligated to get done to appease others or to appease their own misguided sense of trying to be useful. If they get to the end of the day and manage to check off a bunch of stuff from their list, they feel satisfied and productive. They pat themselves on the back and wear their "busy badge" with pride even though they might not have gotten one millimeter closer to their definite purpose that day.

Worse yet, some individuals don't even bother to create a written task list; instead, they attempt to store everything in their mind, continuously juggling tasks and trying to remember all of their appointments in their head. They generally wind up feeling anxious and utterly overwhelmed by the mental load.

Honestly, everyone suffers from task mismanagement in some way, shape, or form. No one on earth is immune to letting the urgent dictate their day or taking on too many things at once to appease others. We're all guilty, including me.

At any particular moment of the day, week, month, or year, we sit on a scale of productivity. When we're disorganized, prioritizing others' needs over our own and reacting impulsively rather than acting with intention, we descend on the scale of productivity. We slide from wealthy living to busy living.

Fortunately, the Law of Priority brings awareness to the behaviors that cause us to slide into busyness so we can perform a rigorous self-audit to see just how far down the scale we've fallen. From there, we can implement strategies to adjust our behavior and move back up the scale toward more time and more wealth.

Time-Rich Mindset: Going at the World

A boy and his horse are walking together through a forest. There's a lot of fog, so visibility is low. Finally, the fog gets so thick that the boy can see almost nothing. So, he comes to a stop.

"What's wrong?" the horse asks.

"I can't see anything in front of me," the boy replies. "There's too much fog!"

"Well, what *can* you see?" the horse asks.

The boy looks down. "I can see my feet."

"Okay, good, you can see your feet," the horse replies. "Can you take one step?"

"Yes, I can take one step," the boy says.

"Great. Take one step," the horse says.

So, the boy takes one step.

"Now take another step," the horse says.

So, the boy takes a second step. In this way, one step at a time, they resume moving through the forest and eventually get where they're going.

It's a simple story that shares an important concept. When we try to focus on too many things, whether steps, tasks, obligations, or ideas, we can easily become overwhelmed, and when we're overwhelmed, it becomes incredibly difficult to make progress. However, if you prioritize the very next step you have to take (or the next task, project, etc.), you can continue making progress.

Don't focus on the 10,000 steps between where you are now and where you want to go. Just prioritize the very next step. And when it's done, prioritize the one after that. And so on.

But you absolutely must start prioritizing tasks that (1) eliminate the unimportant, (2) create leverage, and (3) move you toward your definite purpose. Remember, if you're focused on nothing, you'll be distracted by everything, and if you let tasks clutter up your schedule, they'll clutter up your mind.

As entrepreneur Naval Ravikant famously said, "A busy mind accelerates the perceived passage of time." So, rather than reacting to everything that comes at you, start being intentional about what you allow to take up space in your head and on your schedule each day, each week, and each month. Your time is your most precious commodity, so be ruthless with whom and what you give it to.

I recommend two specific strategies to help you do this. Let's take a look at them both now, then I'll share how I personally implement them in my life.

The Eisenhower Method

The Eisenhower Method is a time management tool that was inspired by a quote from US President Dwight D. Eisenhower, who once said, "I have two kinds of problems, the urgent and the important. The urgent are not important, and the important are never urgent."

This approach uses a simple matrix to help you weigh the importance of any task or project that comes your way. You can find many versions of it online, but in general, it looks something like this:

	Urgent	Not Urgent
Important	Quadrant 1 DO	Quadrant 2 DECIDE
Not Important	Quadrant 3 DELEGATE	Quadrant 4 DELETE

Here's how it works.

Take all of your daily tasks, projects, and obligations and place each of them in one of these four quadrants based on their urgency and importance to achieving your definite purpose.

Tasks that are urgent and important are the ones you should prioritize immediately. These deserve your greatest focus. They may or may not support your definite purpose, but either way, they must be done and usually can't be eliminated. Urgent and important tasks include things that will impede daily life or business health if not done.

For tasks that are important but not urgent, you can decide to do them later. These are tasks that support your definite purpose but don't need to be done right away. Typically, they can be executed during scheduled times that you set aside for "deep work" (i.e., work that requires two to eight hours of focus).

Tasks that are urgent but not important are the most potent time thieves and should be delegated to someone else or automated with a system as soon as possible (as we talked about in the Law of Leverage chapter [5]).

Tasks that are neither urgent nor important are also notorious time pillagers, and they should be ruthlessly eliminated—permanently—from your to-do list (as we discussed in the Law of Elimination chapter [3]).

The Eisenhower Method is a relatively quick and simple exercise you can spend a couple of minutes doing before facing the day. When combined with the next tactic, it will give you a great deal of clarity and help in learning to live your day with absolute intention—without succumbing to overwhelm.

The Ivy Lee Method

Charles Schwab was the president of Bethlehem Steel Corporation in the early twentieth century and one of the richest men in the world. However, he was always looking for ways to improve efficiency and boost productivity. And so, as the story goes, he scheduled a meeting with a productivity consultant by the name of Ivy Lee and said, "Show me a way to get more things done."

"I can do that," Ivy Lee replied. "Just give me 15 minutes with each of your executives."

"How much will this cost me?" Schwab asked.

"It won't cost you anything," Lee replied, "unless my advice works. After three months, if my advice works, you can send me a check for whatever amount of money you feel it's worth."

During those meetings with executives, Ivy Lee shared his own daily routine for achieving peak productivity. It goes like this:

- At the end of each day, write the six most important things you need to accomplish tomorrow. Write no more and no fewer than six.
- Arrange the six things in order of their importance.
- When you get to work tomorrow, focus only on the first and most important task. Work until it is complete. Then move to the second task.
- Tackle the rest of the list in the same way.
- At the end of the day, use any unfinished tasks to create a new list of six tasks for the next day.
- Repeat this process every day.

And that was it. That's the Ivy Lee Method. In the end, this exercise was so effective at boosting productivity that Charles Schwab sent Ivy Lee a check for $25,000 (worth $400,000 in today's money).[1]

Though it sounds simple, the reality is most people don't approach their day with intentionality. They react to tasks as they arise rather than prioritizing and focusing on the most important things. The Ivy Lee Method gives you a super easy way to structure your day so you spend the most time on work that actually matters.

Personally, I keep my prioritized daily task list in the notes section of my phone, pinned to the top so it is readily accessible each day. I call it my "Dominate List" because it makes me feel like I'm dominating my schedule and making efficient use of my time. Creating the list requires some tough decisions, especially because you are limiting yourself to just six things. However, it makes it easier to get started, helps you focus, and prevents multitasking.

When I create my list of six things, I make sure there are always at least a couple of tasks that create leverage and contribute directly to my definite purpose, and I avoid putting things like "get groceries" on my list because I can always delegate that to someone else. Similarly, I avoid putting meetings or appointments on this list. I can make a task to set an appointment or meeting, but the actual meeting itself goes into my digital calendar. Tasks go on your list, but appointments (meetings) go in your digital calendar.

Every morning when I wake up, I look first at my calendar and second at my Dominate List.

< Notes

26 April 2024 at 12:47 PM

DOMINATE LIST:

IMPORTANT & URGENT:

- ○ Upload videos to FB group
- ○ Book Review - send sketches to Ellie
- ○ Call Ian - re AI connection
- ○ Create recognition program for Elite program
- ○ Create side hustle school work book
- ○ Call Adrian re final bank docs

A mentor of mine first showed me the Ivy Lee Method seven or eight years ago, and I've used it ever since. I can tell you from experience that it will make you far more productive than you've ever been. You will no longer feel overwhelmed when facing the day because you know exactly what you're going to work on.

If you have trouble limiting yourself to just six tasks, that's a good sign you need to eliminate some tasks or delegate them to other people or systems. Recruit a virtual assistant. That's a quick way to eliminate at least a few things, and once your virtual assistant is trained, he or she will be able to handle part of your list even while you're sleeping.

In fact, I recommend adding "delegation" to your task list. Make it one of the six things so you focus on off-loading tasks on a daily basis. If you handle six things a day, systems handle six things a day, and other people are handling six things a day, then you're completing eighteen tasks a day without breaking the Ivy Lee Method, and you'll achieve more by doing less. This is how you multiply your time.

Delegate to Your Diary

Your brain is for having ideas, not for storing them. Most people are storing ideas, lists, and tasks in their head all the time, so one objective of a time-rich mindset is to delegate all of that information to

- Your Dominate List (six important and urgent tasks written in the notes of your phone)
- Your Google Calendar (critical meetings, deep work tasks, events, family time, and time for rest)

My personal diary contains every single meeting or event I have to go to. If it's not on my calendar, it's not going to happen. That's a rule I live by. That includes personal downtime, date nights, going to the gym, and client calls and meetings. They all go into my Google Calendar so I can delete them from my head.

This not only forces me to create clarity about my tasks and ruthlessly eliminate the unnecessary every single day (essentially, a task audit) but it also gives me a simple road map to follow toward my definite purpose.

Every morning, I wake up and spend about 30 minutes checking the stock market, reading news, replying to a few messages and simple emails, and "clearing my plate" of low-hanging fruit tasks, but as soon as I'm done with that, I look at two things:

- My Google Calendar—What meetings, events, or important items must I engage in or prepare for today?
- My Dominate List—What critical tasks and important work am I going to spend my time on today to progress myself toward my definite purpose?

It only takes about 30 seconds to read these two things each morning, and they keep me focused, give me the next step to take to be productive, and assist me in alleviating overload and anxiety. This helps me keep things super simple.

Simple scales, complex fails.

One important note: I constantly apply the Time-Rich Laws to my Dominate List and Google Calendar. Busyness is an insidious malady that can infect anyone at any time (including me). The key to inoculating against it is to regularly audit your task list and apply the laws.

During the audit, ask yourself the following:

- Is this task or meeting in alignment with my definite purpose?
- Can I eliminate any tasks, meetings, or events that are unimportant?

- Which tasks can I delegate or automate?
- Which tasks can I bundle together to execute more swiftly?
- What single task on my list, once accomplished, will eliminate the need for many other tasks?
- Which tasks or meetings are a priority right now? Am I just saying yes to fulfill a need to feel busy and important?
- Which tasks will yield the highest return on my time?

For example, if you have "get groceries" on your list, you could put "set up a grocery home-delivery app" on your list and put it at the very top. Why? Because once you complete this task, it will forever eliminate the weekly task of getting groceries.

What I am saying is that it's important to audit your own Dominate List and digital calendar each day to make sure you're not doing things for the sake of doing them. Be ruthless about it! Your job is not to just do tasks but to make as many of them redundant as possible.

By answering these critical questions and auditing your tasks each day, you will stave off most attempts by the busyness bug to infect your time and productivity.

Now, do the strategies I just shared guarantee that you will always be super productive? Well, no, of course not. We are human beings, after all, not human doings. Even when it seems like you have this whole time management thing dialed in, you can still catch a case of the busyness bug.

It happens to me from time to time. Occasionally, I procrastinate, I overcommit, I say yes to too many things, or I lose focus and let others impede my boundaries. You'll never be a perfect time manager, so don't beat yourself up too much when you fail at it. Much like riding a bike, you're bound to fall off now and again.

The key is to revisit the Four Time-Rich Laws and implement them again in your life when you experience feelings of overwhelm, overwork, unfulfillment, or exhaustion from busyness. Only through bold and consistent application of these laws can you reclaim your time and wealth.

The Focus Funnel

I want to share one more tool that can help you prioritize the most important tasks: the Focus Funnel by Rory Vaden.

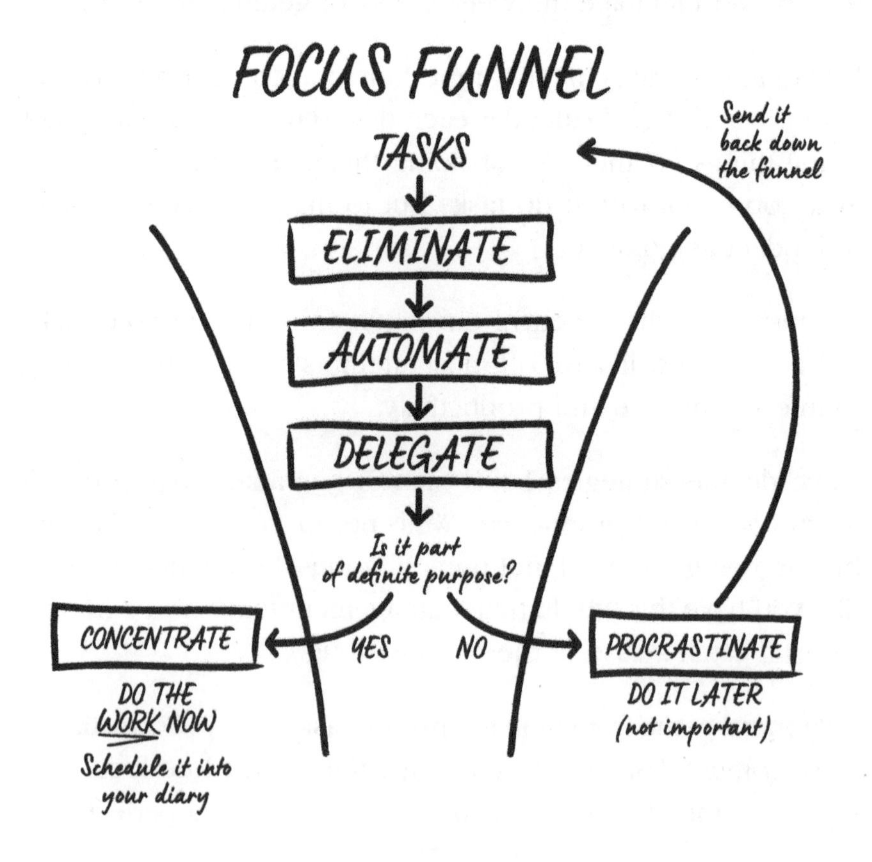

In case the figure isn't self-explanatory, here's how it works. For every task, first ask yourself, *Can I eliminate it?* If you can't, then ask yourself, *Can I automate it by leveraging a system to do it for me?* If you can't, then ask yourself, *Can I delegate it to another person?*

If the answer to all three is no, then go ahead and do it yourself. I would add one more question to the end of the funnel: *Does it support my definite purpose?* If the first three questions are a no and the fourth question is a yes, then (and only then) should you do the task yourself.

Instead of defaulting to doing every task yourself, send it through the Focus Funnel first and see if you can't take it off your to-do list.

The Law of Priority Tactics

First tactic: Apply all of your daily tasks, projects, and obligations to the Eisenhower Method to clarify which ones are (1) urgent and important, (2) important but not urgent, (3) urgent but not important, or (4) neither urgent nor important.

Second tactic: Use the Ivy Lee Method to create a list of the six most important things you need to accomplish tomorrow (your Dominate List).

Third tactic: Begin delegating everything, including personal downtime, date nights, going to the gym, and client calls and meetings, to your digital calendar.

I've used this Focus Funnel method with my clients. On one occasion, we conducted a millionaire immersion day at the Versace Hotel on the Gold Coast. One of the attendees shared her definite purpose to build a coaching business. She had identified her most important tasks as generating leads, booking calls, and making sales. However, she was also working on two books but struggling to finish them.

"I don't know how to get all of this done," she told me. "I need to make sales, but I also need to finish these books. What should I do?"

So, I took all of her tasks through the Focus Funnel. It became very clear that finishing the books had nothing to do with her definite purpose, wouldn't build leverage to grow her business, and wasn't really urgent. Therefore, those tasks could simply be eliminated.

"No more working on the books," I said.

I expected her to be disappointed, but instead, she seemed relieved. It was like a terrible burden had been lifted from her shoulders. She had been given permission to stop working on something that wasn't moving her forward so she could prioritize the things that really mattered.

Another client of mine came to me during one of our monthly coaching sessions at a time when she was overwhelmed with work. She showed me the list of everything she needed to get done in various parts of her business, and I must say, it was an impressive list! She was struggling to figure out which of the tasks to prioritize, so I took every task through the Focus Funnel.

This process made it clear that she was working on the wrong things. She had prioritized tasks like designing booklets and planning events, stuff that could easily be automated or outsourced to other people. What she really needed to focus on was creating referral partners for her business.

So, we reoriented her to-do list, off-loaded most of the things she had been spending time on, and honed in on lead generation. As a result, her business flourished, and ironically, she found she was more productive (but less busy) than ever.

Exercise: Dominate List

I've given you a number of tools to help you prioritize, so let's start with your Dominate List:

- You could use pen and paper, but I recommend using the Notes app on your smartphone instead. That way your list is readily accessible, and it can be tied to your Google Calendar or some other online diary.
- Use the Ivy lee Method to create your six-item Dominate List.
- Use the other techniques in this chapter to determine the relative importance of various tasks. Then stick to your list!
- **Note:** Make sure one of your Dominate List tasks covers "setting up my digital calendar for the week." This will enable you to delegate all of your meetings, appointments, exercise, rest, and leisure times to your digital calendar for the coming week.
- Once you've prioritized your work, set rigid boundaries in your schedule to keep other things from creeping in.

Now, I know some people have trouble setting boundaries, so let's spend Chapter 11 exploring this topic because it's going to be vitally important to your well-being.

> If you would like some help implementing the Law of Priority, head to the back of the book and click the link or scan the QR code to book a free Time Rich coaching session with our team.

Chapter 11

Setting Boundaries

"Be easy to find, hard to reach."

—Codie Sanchez

John Mark Comer is the author of one of my favorite books, *The Ruthless Elimination of Hurry*.[1] In the book, he tells his true life story as a Christian pastor who built one of the largest and most successful churches in North America but, in the process of doing so, lost his soul.

When you're the head of a massive church (or any organization), a whole lot of people want access to your time, and it becomes very easy to fall into the trap of being too available, giving too much of your time, and working without boundaries. This is especially true of pastors because, after all, isn't a church supposed to be built on the value of serving all and giving all you have to others? Isn't that what Jesus did?

Well, not exactly. If you know the Bible, then you probably know that Jesus started each day in solitude. You also know that both the Old Testament and much of the New Testament talk about the sanctity of the Sabbath and the importance of having one day a week for rest and worship rather than work. Heck, we're told in the book of Genesis that even God rested on the seventh day! So, if God could set aside a day to rest, why can't you?

Throughout the book, John makes it clear that the reason he lost his soul was because he did not set firm boundaries. He was too accessible, said yes too often, and took on too many things at once out of a fear of disappointing others or not being loved. By all accounts, he was extremely busy! The result, as he explains, was a feeling of constantly being in a hurry.

Hurry is a symptom of busyness, and hurry is not a place from which we can truly serve or love. As I noted in the first chapter,

Corrie ten Boom, a Holocaust survivor, once said, "If the Devil can't make you sin, he'll make you busy."[2]

Think about all the times you have been short-tempered, all the times you have not been present, all the times you have been stressed. I'll bet most of those instances happened while you were in a hurry. Love and hurry cannot reside together, much like wealth and busyness.

John's story unfolds with him eventually losing his church, losing his soul, and almost losing his family. Finally, he sought advice from his mentor, Pastor Dallas Willard. He asked Dallas, "What is the key to a successful life?"

Dallas replied, "The number one problem you will face is time. People are just too busy to live emotionally healthy, rich, vibrant lives. Therefore, you must ruthlessly eliminate hurry from your life. There is nothing else."[3]

Taking this sage advice, John began to fiercely protect his time, eliminate various commitments he'd made, and slowly diminish the level of hurry in his life. He set boundaries and applied the Law of Elimination to give his soul the time it needed to catch up to his body.

Time-Poor Mindset: Easy to Find, Easy to Reach

Do you find yourself agreeing to tasks out of fear of being impolite or unpopular? Do you often take on responsibilities reluctantly just because you crave the validation of being needed? Are you constantly rushing, feeling like you're perpetually short on time? If any of these sound familiar, chances are you struggle with setting boundaries in your life.

Let me ask you a question. What would happen if you made yourself less readily available? What if you didn't respond to every message or notification the moment it pops up? Would the world stop turning? Would you become irrelevant? Would people stop liking you? These worries might nag at you—and trust me, I understand how tough it can be to break free from this cycle—but here's the thing: more often than not, these fears never come to fruition.

People with a time-poor mindset feel obligated to "rescue" others all the time, take on their tasks, accept all invitations, be very easy to contact, and say yes to just about everything.

This behavior, which most of us have displayed at one time or another, stems from a yearning to be needed or loved. It gives us a feeling of significance, which is a powerful driver of human behavior. We don't want to disappoint people, and we strongly believe that our contribution is needed. As a result, we make ourselves too accessible, too available, too easy to reach. It may make us feel desired, but it's actually doing us (and others) more harm than we realize.

There is a Newtonian law in physics that states, "For every action, there is an equal and opposite reaction," which is precisely what occurs when we are at everyone's beck and call. The first action (saying yes to everyone) causes our own time and our own important goals to slip through our fingers. Moreover, if this action is not reciprocated by the opposing party, then we often become resentful and exhausted, which is exactly what happened to John Mark Comer in the story of his church.

The opposing action, though, is equally damaging, not only to us but to the other party we're aiming to help. Being quick to help at the first sign of struggle denies other parties a chance to solve the problem on their own and can lead to overdependence, entitlement, and a low sense of self worth in that individual.

Have you ever seen the consequences of an overprotective parents? It's not just exhausting for the parents; it's damaging to the children in terms of their growth and development. The same can be said for friends, employees, partners, and a spouse. If you are too accessible, too available, and too fast to solve their problems, they will not grow as independent leaders or effective problem solvers.

This lose-lose situation is precisely why airlines tell you that in case of emergency, you should put your own oxygen mask on first before helping others, even your own children. Because if you can't get the oxygen you need, you may not be able to help others get what they need.

For sure, it can be difficult to say no to loved ones, it's going to be hard to stop "rescuing" people all the time, and it'll be hard to put your oxygen mask on first (especially if you're a parent), but it's important to break this pattern. Doing so will not only win you back your time but also it will give others the chance to develop and grow too. Remember, my delegation is your personal development.

The same can be said for setting boundaries. By setting firm boundaries, you not only win back your time but you also give others a chance to be their own heroes—a great win-win outcome!

There was a time in my life when I found myself struggling with boundaries, constantly in a hurry, seemingly at everyone's beck and call. I was afraid if I didn't assert my input constantly and quickly into everything, our businesses would fall apart, our income wouldn't grow, and people would hate me. This was, of course, driven by an inflated sense of self-importance. I was attaching my activity to our outcomes and mistaking busy for wealthy. As a result, I found myself suffering from a terrible bout of hurry sickness.

As Alisha pointed out, even when I sat down to "rest," one of my legs would be vigorously shaking, as I struggled to cope with the anxiety and stress I'd put myself under. She was also the first person to point out that my instant replies to our consultants was fostering a culture of dependence on us (she is very clever, Alisha is). I'd said yes to too many things and was too quick to respond out of a fear of not being productive and not being valued, and as a result, I found myself in a constant hurry, all the time, every day.

Eventually, I picked up John Mark Comer's book, and I took to heart everything he had to say. After implementing some of his suggestions to eliminate hurry from my life, I began to feel a sense of peace wash over me. It was as if someone had given me permission to become wealthy but to do it peacefully. The hustle-and-grind paradigm that I'd been depending on to create success now seemed more like a hindrance than an advantage. I had mistakenly developed the idea that "busy" equaled "wealthy," but my mission now was to interrupt this old pattern and rectify my behavior.

Time-Rich Mindset: Easy to Find, Hard to Reach

I am a highly ambitious person, so curing a bad bout of hurry sickness caused by a chronic infection from the busyness bug was not an easy task for me. I knew I had to set some boundaries and end the paradigm that being busy was the same as getting wealthy, but I wasn't sure how to do it.

Ultimately, the answer was found in my own behavior. I realized I was the root cause of my busyness, so I had to figure out which aspects of my life put me in that state of mind. Then I had to tactically set boundaries in place that would lead to new behaviors. My objective was to stay productive but become less busy and, thereby, cure my hurry sickness.

Here are the five tactical steps I took to reclaim my time and attention and rescue my hurried soul.

Be Easy to Find, Hard to Reach

When you earn a certain level of success (in almost any area of life), you become more sought after, more people desire your attention, and due to smartphones, social media, email, and dozens of instant messaging apps, your attention has never been easier to get. In fact, it has become really hard to ignore people.

Human beings are social animals, so deep down we all yearn for validation from our peers. This yearning for connection and acceptance from others drives us to respond to every text, call, message, ping, or ring as soon as we can. When few people are seeking our attention, this isn't a problem, but when our attention is in high demand, it quickly becomes overwhelming.

So, what's the cure? Most of us don't want to come across as arrogant, rude, or unwelcoming.

This first cure comes from Codie Sanchez: "Be easy to find, but hard to reach."

In other words, provide value to the world, be omnipresent, promote yourself, and shine a bright light, but don't be so accessible to everyone. Set some firm boundaries. Don't react to every attempt from others to get your attention.

Here are a few simple rules I follow that make me harder to reach:

- **I don't answer phone calls except from direct family.** Actually, I have a voicemail message that clearly states, "I don't answer calls, so please hang up and text me." This prevents interruptions throughout the day but also gives the person calling the opportunity to solve their own problem first. With so many communication options these days, calling someone unprompted and uninvited really does feel like committing time robbery.
- **I read emails but seldom reply.** Using people leverage, I have my assistant reply to the most urgent emails.
- **I am more careful not to respond immediately to "cries for help"** (or what we like to call "just a quick one" messages).

- **I keep all notifications turned off on my phone.** In fact, I have moved all of my social media apps to the very end screen of my phone so they are difficult to see. I have also deleted the Facebook Messenger app entirely so it's harder to check.
- **I don't often seek or accept "coffee dates" or requests to "pick my brain."** Yes, even from clients. These days, interaction is usually done at a scheduled in-person event or via Zoom. The only exceptions are direct family and close friends.

If It's Not a "Hell Yes," Then It's a No

When I was younger, I could eat junk food all I wanted and not put on an ounce of fat. I seemed to be immune to its damaging effects. Over time, I developed a taste (and a hard-to-break habit) for junk food. This became a problem by my early thirties, when even a glimpse of a KFC chicken burger would put fat on me.

The problem is that, as the old saying goes, "The chains of habit are too light to be felt before they are too heavy to be broken." It becomes much harder to give up behaviors that have served us so well for so long. The same can be said for saying yes to every invitation or opportunity. When you're young, you're trying to build a network, a business, and a ton of skills, and you yearn for opportunity. To create as many opportunities as you can, it makes sense to say yes to almost everything.

However, as you become more successful, you begin to find yourself doing things, going places, and experiencing things that don't bring you any joy or move you toward your definite purpose. Ultimately, saying yes to everything becomes a bad habit. Entrepreneur Alex Hormozi summed this up well: "Everything you say yes to is saying no to the thing you say you want most. So you have to say no until it hurts. Then say no some more. So you can take one yes all the way."[4] Alex understands the concept of opportunity cost. He knows that when you say yes to one thing, you say no to everything else.

To combat the old habit of saying yes to everything and finding ourselves caught up in events or projects that bring us no value, as we discussed in Chapter 3, Alisha and I use a tactic we learned from Derek Sivers called "Hell Yes or No."

The tactic is simple. If we are invited somewhere, asked to join a project or opportunity, or have the chance to get involved in an activity, Alisha and I will look at each other and ask, "Is it a hell yes?" In other words, is it something that we really, *really* want to do? If the answer is not a resounding "Hell yes," then it's a simple no.

This is why you will no longer find us snorkeling on vacation, or find me sitting in a musical, or find us involved in every single business opportunity that comes across our desk. Remember, no is a complete sentence. When you first apply this tactic, it should feel uncomfortable, but stick to your guns. When the initial guilt fades, you will be rewarded with a feeling of liberation and relief.

Make the Decision to Own Your Time

By now, you've likely grasped the efficiency boost that comes from delegating tasks to your electronic calendar. It's a simple truth: if it's not scheduled, chances are it won't happen. As Jocko Willink, a former US Navy SEAL and leadership consultant, aptly puts it, "Discipline equals freedom."[5] But let's take it a step further. I've been using an electronic calendar for years, but it wasn't until I embraced the concept of a "default diary" that I truly began to own my time.

A wise business coach introduced me to this concept. He said that although important meetings and events should certainly always be scheduled, I should also prioritize my own commitments before other people snagged those time slots. So, I began prescheduling specific blocks in my week dedicated to deep, focused work on various projects.

This simple adjustment empowered me to take control of my time. His lesson was invaluable: "If you don't structure your week, someone else will do it for you."

Expanding on this idea, I started theming my days (after Alisha cleverly suggested it a dozen times) based on the type of work I needed to tackle. Instead of bouncing from meetings, deep work sessions, tasks, coaching, to appointments haphazardly, I allocated specific days for specific types of tasks.

For instance, Mondays became dedicated to our network marketing business, and Tuesdays were reserved for content creation and deep work. Wednesdays and Thursdays are for student coaching, and Friday is generally wide open for me to decide what I wish to work on. I prefer to keep weekends for family time and rest, though I do make exceptions for running and attending events that are aligned with our businesses and my definite purpose, which rarely feels like work.

My calendar used to be packed with back-to-back sales calls, early morning and late evening team meetings, client appointments, and endless tasks. However, once I started leveraging people and systems, running a default diary, and "theming" my days, my digital diary began to open up, enabling me to prioritize the work that truly mattered to me.

Schedule Solitude, Rest, and Play

Meditation, it's like trying to hug a cactus. There, I said it. Now, don't get me wrong, if you're all about that Zen life, good for you! But for me, it's not my cup of tea. I've given it a shot, but let's just say my mind wanders off faster than a toddler in a candy store.

The closest thing I have to traditional meditation is something performance coach Nam Baldwin taught me, which he calls *mind defragging*. It's like putting your brain from "drive" into "neutral." How does it work? It's actually quite simple. You breathe in deeply for five seconds, then breathe out for five seconds; rinse and repeat five times. Think of it like a mini-meditation that you can do anywhere, anytime. Give it a whirl. It's like hitting the snooze button on your brain. I use it to calm myself before training events, before bedtime to fall asleep faster, or even just to give my brain a chance to be more creative.

As simple as this method is, we also need time for solitude. I understand that as well. I need a time when I can be by myself to think, pray, and be creative. Apart from taking a shower, I find time for solitude when I'm walking to the gym. It's a 10-minute walk both ways, so I spend that time enjoying the warm sun and listening to music. I resist the urge to look at my phone during that time (as well as when I'm at the gym).

This is by far my most creative time each day. I used to schedule it into my diary, but it has become such an important daily ritual that I now use it as a reward after a morning of work.

My routine might not work for you, so find your own form of meditation, your own way to "defrag" your mind and eliminate hurry from your life. This is often called *mindfulness*, but it's really just a matter of becoming aware of your own hurried thoughts and bringing yourself back to the present moment. However you do this, it doesn't have to be fancy. In fact, we can start being mindful in small ways.

For example, when I was deep in the throes of hurry sickness, I would walk fast, read fast, drive fast, go to the bathroom fast, and even brush my teeth fast! But now when I start to do any of these things too fast, I catch myself and make a point of slowing down. Yes, I have even begun mindfully brushing my teeth more slowly.

When I walk to the gym, I mindfully slow down my pace so I can take time to admire my surroundings and smell the roses (metaphorically speaking, of course, because there are no roses along the path to and from the gym). People pray, worship, or give thanks in their own unique ways. This is how I do it.

Slowing your pace doesn't speed things up, but it does slow down time. When we slow time down, we tend to make fewer mistakes. Personally, I've found that I also develop better ideas, and I am generally a happier person.

The US Navy SEALs have a famous saying about productivity: "Slow is smooth, and smooth is fast." I practice this motto as often as I can.

If you have a clear definite purpose, boldly eliminate the unnecessary, delegate swiftly to people and systems to carry out urgent and repeatable tasks, and prioritize and schedule important work within appropriate boundaries in your life, then why on earth would you ever be in a hurry?

Manage Your Energy

If you've ever boxed or sparred, you know how exhausted you get in the ring if you're tense, move too much, and miss punches. The lactic acid and fatigue that can set in after only sixty seconds are nothing short of excruciating. So, if there's one thing I learned from my mate Gavin, training for my first boxing fight back in 2019, it was to manage my energy in the ring. Now, as I get older, I find it's equally important to manage my energy outside the ring so I can optimize my productivity and time.

How do I do that? Simple. I use a system, specifically an app called RISE, to track my two daily energy peaks along with my sleep.

We all experience two distinct energy peaks and dips per day. That's one thing I learned from using this app. I also learned just how tired I truly was because the app showed me how much sleep debt I'd accumulated by not making it a priority. What I love about the app is that it gamifies my sleep, and it shows me when I will be most productive during the day. That enables me to plan both my work and rest more efficiently in my digital calendar (yes, it syncs up to my digital calendar).

I know now that my energy peaks are between 10 a.m. and 12 p.m. (morning peak) and between 5 p.m. and 7 p.m. (evening peak), so I do my best to schedule my deep, focused work or online events during these times. As I write this paragraph, it's 9:30 in the morning, and I know I'll be at maximum energy for the next two hours, so I'm hard at deep work writing this very book.

Conversely, I schedule Zoom meetings, gym work, or life admin, which don't need as much focus, during the energy dips. This helps me to optimize my production for the day to achieve more than I would without taking this data onboard.

The app also alerts me not to take caffeine any time after 11:30 a.m. (a great boundary) so I can fall asleep more easily at night. This has made a huge difference to the quality of my sleep.

Finally, it alerts me when my melatonin levels are at their peak, which means if I hit the pillow and close my eyes during this "melatonin window" and take my five-by-five deep breaths, my chances of getting a great sleep are maximized. Does it always go to plan? No. During travels, I have racked up some pretty serious sleep debt on the app. Still, it has forced me to focus on my rest, sleep, and energy levels, thereby enabling me to achieve my goals with less effort each day. The compound effect of this has been incredibly powerful, and becoming energy rich has helped me become time rich.

Setting Boundaries Tactics

First tactic: Dare to make yourself less accessible. Set some boundaries by not responding immediately to every "cry for help" through phone calls, text messages, emails, and social media.

Second tactic: When faced with an event or project, practice "Hell Yes or No" to decide if you will get involved or accept the invitation.

Third tactic: Begin structuring your week through a "default diary" and schedule time for solitude, rest, and play.

Fourth tactic: Download the RISE app and begin managing your energy and sleep.

Feeling Overwhelmed

One of my mentorship students came to me feeling overwhelmed. He had full-time work and three side businesses to run, and he was also married with three kids. With such a substantial workload, it wasn't surprising that he was running on empty.

He sought my guidance on how to maintain balance in his life between his relationships and his businesses. I asked if he had set aside time for rest, date nights, or moments of relaxation in his calendar. He admitted he hadn't, so I encouraged him to start allocating dedicated quality time for specific activities throughout the week.

As I explained, if an activity, including rest, isn't designated in your calendar, it tends to get overlooked. Other demands on your time will creep in and take over. You absolutely must incorporate designated times for hanging out with your spouse and children as well as periods of rest.

I told him, "When activities are scheduled, they are more likely to happen." Using my own example, I shared that on Mondays, I intentionally allocate four to five hours for doing nothing serious until midday, embracing the freedom without any sense of guilt.

By applying the Law of Priority, I helped him whip his calendar into shape, and he wholeheartedly embraced it. Now, he has more time to relax, he has more time with his family, and he no longer gets burned out or feels overwhelmed with tasks.

Exercise: Leveraging Systems to Create Boundaries

Okay, it's time to create some boundaries and introduce a bit of structure into your calendar. Put a stop to the burnout and overwhelm.

- **First:** I recommend downloading the RISE app. This simple app helps you improve your sleeping and rest habits so you have more energy throughout the day. It's easy to use and won't demand too much of your time.
- **Second:** If you haven't already, download and start using Google Calendar and your Notes app. Structure your weekly schedule with regular, predictable time slots for work, rest, personal time, and family time. Create rigid boundaries in your calendar so you can always say no. Don't be afraid to make yourself unavailable to other people!

- **Third:** Consider turning off notifications on all of your apps and moving your social media apps to the very last screen of your smartphone. That way you won't see the little notification numbers in the corner of the app icons. All of these little apps, especially social media, want your constant attention. They want you to interact with them all the time. Remember your hourly rate. Is social media really worth your hourly rate? Probably not, so create obstacles that prevent apps from demanding your time.

These three tactics are a good way to start creating some rigid boundaries in your schedule so you can prioritize the most important things. A lot of people and things are trying to steal your time and energy. Protect yourself! Protect your time! Manage your energy. Otherwise, you're never going to make real progress toward your definite purpose.

Becoming Time Rich Starts Today

It has been said that if you took all the money in the world and handed it out equally to every person, in just a few years it would find its way back to exactly where it is today. Why? Because wealth is not an accident but the result of applying a particular set of guiding financial principles to your behavior—principles that have been around since the ancient days of Babylon. They are not new, and frankly, they are widely known.

So, why isn't everyone wealthy? Because most people can't manage their own behavior well enough to follow them.

The same can be said about time.

There are some people who seem to float through life with an abundance of free time and wealth and others who quite literally slave away and sacrifice every minute of freedom they have just to make a few extra dollars to pay the next rent bill. The difference between the two is merely a decision to change.

My wish for you is that you will make this change, apply the laws from this book, and start winning back the most precious commodity you have: your time.

To do so will require a decision from you to consistently apply the **Four Time-Rich Laws** to your life:

1. **The Law of Definite Purpose:** Take ownership of your destiny by cultivating a vivid mental map of the fulfilling life you hope to achieve in five to 10 years. Then maintain an unwavering motivation and focus on getting there.
2. **The Law of Elimination:** Less is more. Chip away all the unnecessary tasks, obligations, and stuff in your life so you can curate a life that resonates with your definite purpose rather than mere busyness.
3. **The Law of Leverage:** Leverage people, partnerships, systems, and capital in order to achieve more by doing less.
4. **The Law of Priority:** Audit your to-do list vigorously each day to focus on the important, not simply the urgent. Establish rigid boundaries in your calendar so you're less accessible. Fiercely protect your time and energy. Ruthlessly eliminate hurry from your life.

If you will apply these four laws, I promise you will find that you have far more time, more freedom, and more flexibility, while at the same time achieving far more than you ever could before.

But of course, it's easy to feel overwhelmed when you finish a book like this. You may be thinking, *How do I even begin to apply these laws to my everyday life?* So, to ensure that you don't just finish this book and go back to the same old time-poor behaviors, I want to give you some actionable steps to take—starting today.

Time-Rich Tactics: Checklist

- ☐ Craft a one-paragraph essay that describes your desired life five to 10 years from now. This is the definite purpose you're going to work toward. Curb all distractions.
- ☐ Write a list of the top ten things you are currently working on. Do it quickly, within 30 seconds. Once you're done, pause for 10 seconds, then cross out all of the tasks on the list except for the most important three. Focus on doing these three things *exclusively*.
- ☐ Start putting items up for sale on Facebook Marketplace.
- ☐ Use the money to invest into cash-producing assets (e.g., stocks or real estate) or as seed money for a business that will generate passive income (e.g., a network marketing business).
- ☐ Figure out your hourly rate by taking your gross annual income, dividing it by 52 weeks in the year, and then dividing the result by 20 hours in a week.
- ☐ Create three lists, labeled "Can't Do," "Shouldn't Do," and "Don't Want to Do." Then place each task or responsibility in your life into one of these three lists.
- ☐ Figure out how much it would cost to pay someone to do each of these tasks for you, then outsource everything that costs less than your hourly rate.
- ☐ Look on websites such as www.upwork.com, www.fiverr.com, and www.airtasker.com to find someone who will do these tasks for you.
- ☐ Use "Do, Document, Delegate" to make sure that any task you outsource is done correctly so you can truly let go of it.

- ☐ Consider forming a collaborative partnership with someone who has the time, energy, network, skills, and money that you lack.
- ☐ Stop going to the grocery store. Instead, download an app for a local grocery store and set up weekly deliveries to begin leveraging systems and people to do basic work for you.
- ☐ Set up Google Calendar on your phone and schedule in meetings, work time, rest, and leisure.
- ☐ Move some of your in-person meetings to Zoom.
- ☐ Make sure you have active profiles on Facebook, Instagram, and whatever other relevant social media platforms there are at the time you're reading this. Start posting things and connecting with people.
- ☐ Download ChatGPT (chat.openai.com). Watch some YouTube videos on how to use it, then start testing it for creating your social media posts, marketing content, and whatever else you might need.
- ☐ Open an account on a micro-investing app and put $10 in it. Invest that $10 in an index fund.
- ☐ Instead of buying the next big material possession, invest the money into the index fund—make this an ongoing habit.
- ☐ Use the Ivy Lee Method to create a Dominate List composed of six tasks that you're going to tackle tomorrow (no more than six).
- ☐ Tomorrow morning, start with the first task and focus on it exclusively until it's done. Then move to the second task. And so on.

- ☐ Download the RISE app and use it to improve your sleeping and rest habits so you have more energy throughout the day.
- ☐ Begin structuring your weekly schedule with regular, predictable time slots for work, rest, personal time, and family time. Create rigid boundaries in your digital calendar so you can always say no. Put the word *something* in your diary. Don't be afraid to be unavailable to people.

Embracing a new paradigm is always challenging. It can be hard to let go of the old mindset that busyness leads to wealth. I get that. However, the exercises I've given you will help you take action to form a new paradigm.

Remember, the message at the heart of everything I've shared is this: if you scale your time, you will scale your wealth. Don't focus solely on trying to create money. Rather, focus on creating more time for yourself, and you will bring in more money.

And, after all, isn't it *time* to finally get out of the rat race?

Haven't you been stuck in the grind long enough?

Aren't you ready to start achieving more by doing less?

There's nothing I've done to create my life of ultimate freedom that you can't do yourself.

I've given you some initial steps to take, but the most important part is implementation. So, take action! As the old saying goes, "Ignorance on fire is better than knowledge on ice!"

Applying the Four Time-Rich Laws will radically transform your life and catapult you toward your definite purpose faster than you ever thought possible. I know because it happened to me, and if it happened to me, it can happen to you.

To your success,
Lloyd

P.S. If you've enjoyed this book and would like some help implementing the principles we've covered, I encourage you to book in a *free* Time Rich coaching session with our team.

Scan the QR code or click on this link: www.freecoachingsessions .com

Notes

Chapter 1: The Origins of Busyness

1. GIG-OS, "A Billionaire's Ideas: 5 Tips to Learn from John Rockefeller," Medium, January 2, 2017, https://gig-os.medium.com/a-billionaires-ideas-5-tips-to-learn-from-john-rockefeller-c77c2c8ff21b.
2. Drake Baer, "When Did Busy Become Cool?," Medium, May 23, 2017, https://medium.com/thrive-global/when-did-busy-become-cool-8ca13f5f54f9.

Chapter 2: First Law

1. Irene Pine, "How Bruce Lee Outlined His Plan to Become America's First 'Oriental Super Star'—and Earn US$10 Million—in 1969," *Style*, September 12, 2019, https://www.scmp.com/magazines/style/news-trends/article/3026844/how-bruce-lees-1969-handwritten-plan-be-highest-paid.
2. Robert Greene, *Mastery* (New York: Penguin, 2013), 27.

Chapter 3: Second Law

1. Ichiro Kishimi and Fumitake Koga, *The Courage to Be Disliked* (New York: Simon & Schuster, 2024).
2. Eva M. Krockow, "How Many Decisions Do We Make Each Day?," *Stretching Theory* (blog), *Psychology Today*, September 27, 2018, https://www.psychologytoday.com/us/blog/stretching-theory/201809/how-many-decisions-do-we-make-each-day.

Chapter 4: The Elimination of Stuff

1. Morgan Housel, *The Psychology of Money: Timeless Lessons on Wealth, Greed, and Happiness* (Hampshire, UK: Harriman House, 2020), 70.
2. Winston Churchill, "House of Commons Rebuilding," House of Commons Debates, October 28, 1943, https://api.parliament.uk/historic-hansard/commons/1943/oct/28/house-of-commons-rebuilding#S5CV0393P0_19431028_HOC_283.

Chapter 5: Third Law

1. *Encyclopaedia Britannica*, "Who Built the Pyramids of Giza?," Britannica, accessed June 20, 2024, https://www.britannica.com/video/226777/did-enslaved-people-build-the-pyramids.

Chapter 6: People Leverage

1. Napoleon Hill, *Think and Grow Rich* (New York: TarcherPerigee, 2007), 60.
2. Hill, *Think and Grow Rich*, 81.
3. Dan Sullivan and Benjamin Hardy, *Who Not How: The Formula to Achieve Bigger Goals through Accelerating Teamwork* (Carlsbad, CA: Hay House, 2020).

Chapter 8: Systems Leverage

1. Michael Gerber, *The E-Myth Revisited* (New York: HarperBusiness, 2004), 85.

Chapter 9: Capital Leverage

1. "The Shortness of Time," Farnam Street (blog), accessed June 12, 2024, https://fs.blog/seneca-on-the-shortness-of-time.

Chapter 10: The Fourth Law

1. James Clear, "The Ivy Lee Method: The Daily Routine Experts Recommend for Peak Productivity," accessed June 20, 2024, https://jamesclear.com/ivy-lee.

Chapter 11: Setting Boundaries

1. John Mark Comer, *The Ruthless Elimination of Hurry: How to Stay Emotionally Healthy and Spiritually Alive in the Chaos of the Modern World* (Colorado Springs, CO: WaterBrook, 2019).
2. Comer, *The Ruthless Elimination of Hurry*, 25.
3. Comer, *The Ruthless Elimination of Hurry*, 24.
4. Alex Hormozi, "Most People Underestimate the Things They Have to Say No to When Building," LinkedIn, February 1, 2024, https://www.linkedin.com/posts/alexhormozi_most-people-underestimate-the-things-they-activity-7158836414934065152-n3O8/.
5. Jocko Willink, *Discipline Equals Freedom* (New York: St. Martin's Press, 2021).

Chapter 10: The Fourth Law

Acknowledgments

Books don't write themselves (sadly). It takes a team of great people to bring one together. As such, I'd like to take a moment to thank a few great human beings for the contributions they have made to bring this book to life.

To my incredible (and amazing—oh, and beautiful) wife, Alisha, for her constant encouragement and support (and proofreading) over the last 18 months. But mostly for her steadfast commitment to detail, always applying the *slight edge* in everything we do.

To Jay and his team at Lion Social for getting right behind this vision from the very start and for introducing the Scribe Media team to our project in 2023. I could not ask for a better partner in our education business than Jay. I am indebted to him for his wisdom and contribution.

To Dain Walker who introduced us to Wiley & Sons, which led to a publishing deal, and to Brian and the Team at Wiley & Sons for their support in publishing this book.

To my sister (who is a reading fanatic), who helped with final proofreading. Thank you for your contribution to the book and to our online business career.

To Ellie, Jeff, Michael, and the entire team as Scribe Media for helping write, design, manage, and deliver a book I am deeply proud of.

To my parents, friends, coaches, and mentors who have passed on their wisdom and taught me the various lessons I've shared with you in this book. I see farther because I stand on your shoulders.

About the Author

Lloyd James Ross is the founder and director of Money Buys Happiness LLC, a leading company in financial education, business coaching, and events.

In his early years, Lloyd earned a degree in biomedical science, a master's in international business, and a Juris Doctor. By the age of 23 years old, he was admitted to the Supreme Court of Queensland as a lawyer. He then obtained a full real estate license and worked in commercial sales and leasing before moving to Yas Island, Abu Dhabi, in 2008. There, he assisted in the development of the Grand Prix Circuit, Ferrari World theme park, various residential development master plans, and the Links Golf Course residential project. During his time in Abu Dhabi and Dubai, Lloyd completed Levels I and II of the CFA charter exams and began building a seven-figure share portfolio.

Returning to Australia in 2012, Lloyd partnered with his father to successfully revitalize a 30-year-old family business in property investing, marketing, and sales. He then went on to launch highly successful ventures in both network and digital marketing. He is celebrated as a Two Comma Club award-winner by Clickfunnels.com and holds the prestigious title of Legacy Club Millionaire with Isagenix LLC.

Additionally, he hosts the acclaimed podcast *Money Grows on Trees*, which has garnered well over 155-star reviews and over 430,000 downloads by the end of 2024.

Lloyd is the author of *Money Grows on Trees* and *Money Buys Happiness* and is an experienced international platform speaker, captivating audiences of over 7,000 with his inspiring keynotes. He runs a successful events business and a chain of brick-and-mortar enterprises. Beyond his professional life, Lloyd has won an ICN natural bodybuilding competition, finished the grueling 111-kilometer Guzzler ultramarathon, won and lost exhibition boxing matches, and motorcycled across the Indian Himalayas, among other adventures. He is a devoted husband to his beautiful wife, Alisha, and a proud father to their charming sausage dog, Elvis. In his free time, he enjoys writing books, traveling the world, and managing a personal multimillion-dollar share portfolio.

Index